101 GAMES

TO PLAY BEFORE YOU GROW UP

Exciting and fun games to play anywhere!

Wanna play a game? People have been asking this question as long as there have been people. The ancient Romans played a game similar to backgammon (see page 114), and game boards have been found in ancient burial sites in Egypt. Games don't just bring fun and joy into our lives; they teach us about cooperation; perseverance; and how to strategize, use our bodies, and win and lose with grace.

This book collects 101 of the world's best games. Whatever your mood, there's a game in this book for you—from races, tag, and ball games to cards, board games, and paper and pencil games. Flipping through the pages, you'll find your favorites as well as some you've never heard of!

Quarto
Knows

Inspiring | Educating | Creating | Entertaining

Brimming with creative inspiration, how-to projects, and useful information to enrich your everyday life, Quarto Knows is a favorite destination for those pursuing their interests and passions. Visit our site and dig deeper with our books into your area of interest: Quarto Creates, Quarto Cooks, Quarto Homes, Quarto Lives, Quarto Drives, Quarto Explores, Quarto Gifts, or Quarto Kids.

© 2018 Quarto Publishing Group USA Inc.

First Published in 2018 by Walter Foster Jr., an imprint of The Quarto Group.
6 Orchard Road, Suite 100, Lake Forest, CA 92630, USA.
T (949) 380-7510 **F** (949) 380-7575 **www.QuartoKnows.com**

Walter Foster Jr. titles are also available at discount for retail, wholesale, promotional, and bulk purchase. For details, contact the Special Sales Manager by email at specialsales@quarto.com or by mail at The Quarto Group, Attn: Special Sales Manager, 401 Second Avenue North, Suite 310, Minneapolis, MN 55401 USA.

ISBN: 978-1-63322-337-0

Written by Joe Rhatigan
Illustrated by Diego Vaisberg

Printed in China
10 9 8 7 6 5 4 3

101 GAMES
TO PLAY BEFORE YOU GROW UP

Each entry in this book features rules, tips on playing, fun facts, and other games to try.

So grab a sibling, a friend or two, and even a parent, and try them all!

Use the bottom of the page to rate each game after you play it!

WRITTEN BY JOE RHATIGAN
ILLUSTRATED BY DIEGO VAISBERG

Table of Contents

GAME NO.

1

Rock, Paper, Scissors

AGE LEVEL:
7 and up

NUMBER OF PLAYERS:
2 or more

WHAT YOU NEED:
Your hands

WHERE TO PLAY:
Anywhere

ACTIVITY LEVEL:
Light

THE POINT OF THE GAME:
Produce the strongest element to win

Can't decide who gets the last cookie or who gets to choose the next game to play? Don't flip a coin—it's more fun to play a quick round of Rock, Paper, Scissors.

How to Play

1. Face your opponent. Hold one hand flat, palm up. You'll use your other hand to make the shape you choose.

2. On the count of three, show your shape. Rock is a fist, paper is a flat hand, and scissors is two fingers. Here's what beats what:

   a. Rock beats scissors (a rock can crush metal)

   b. Scissors beats paper (scissors can cut paper)

   c. Paper beats rock (paper can cover a rock)

3. Did you both pick the same shape? Go again, until there's a winner!

What Else to Play

A spin-off of Rock, Paper, Scissors called "Rock, Paper, Scissors, Lizard, Spock" was mentioned in the TV show *The Big Bang Theory*. In this version, lizard can eat paper and poison Spock, but is beat by scissors or rock. Spock can beat scissors or rock, but gets defeated by lizard or paper.

Did You Know?

This game is popular all over the world and has many different variations. In Korea, there's one called *Muk-jji-ppa*, in Japan there's *Yakyuken*, and in Singapore they have *Ji gu pa*.

Played it! ☐ Rating: ☆☆☆☆☆

Date: ___ / ___ / _____

With: _____

Notes: _____

_____

Thumb Wrestling

Also known as thumb war, this game is a miniature version of real wrestling (except you just use your thumb). You can play with a friend while waiting in line, at recess, during car rides, or whenever you're bored. Create tournaments with family and friends, and keep track of your records.

How to Play

1. Face your opponent, and grab each other's right hand.
2. Count down by saying this rhyme: "One, two, three, four, I declare a thumb war." Your thumbs can dance around each other while you chant.
3. After you finish the chant, try to press down your opponent's thumb by using only your thumb. Catch or pin down your opponent's thumb for as long as it takes you to say, "One, two, three, four. I win the thumb war."

Did You Know?

There are official Thumb Wrestling tournaments held all over the world.

What Else to Play

There is such a thing as toe wrestling that's just like arm wrestling, but with your feet. There is also Finger Jousting; two players stand and clasp hands as if they're about to arm wrestle, but with their index fingers sticking out. The goal is to poke your opponent.

Played it! ☐ Rating: ☆☆☆☆☆
Date: ___/___/_____
With: _____
Notes: _____
_____

AGE LEVEL:
6 and up

NUMBER OF PLAYERS:
2

WHAT YOU NEED:
Your hands

WHERE TO PLAY:
Anywhere

ACTIVITY LEVEL:
Light

THE POINT OF THE GAME:
Pin your opponent's thumb

GAME NO.

3

Dictionary

AGE LEVEL:
7 and up

NUMBER OF PLAYERS:
4 or more

WHAT YOU NEED:
Dictionary, paper, pencils

WHERE TO PLAY:
Anywhere

ACTIVITY LEVEL:
Minimal

THE POINT OF THE GAME:
Come up with the most plausible definitions of obscure words

Dictionary isn't so much about defining hard-to-pronounce words, but more about coming up with creative definitions that other players believe are correct. Put on your best poker face and start lying!

How to Play

1. Give each player an identical piece of paper.

2. Choose one player to pick an obscure word from the dictionary—a word no one will know—and announce the word to the rest of the players. If another player knows what the word means, have the first player choose another word.

3. Each player then writes a possible definition for the word. The definitions can be silly, serious, or a little of both. The goal is to create a definition that everyone else thinks is the real meaning of the word. Meanwhile, the player that chose the word writes down the actual definition.

4. When finished, fold all the definitions in half and give them to the first player to shuffle and read aloud. The players vote for the definition they believe is correct. (The first player does not get a vote.)

5. Players earn one point if they vote for the correct definition and one point for each vote they receive for their imaginary definition.

Tip

The player that chooses the word should review the definitions carefully before reading them aloud. Stumbling over someone's writing is a sure sign that a definition isn't the correct one … unless the player stumbles on purpose!

The player that chose the word earns three points if no one chooses the correct definition.

6. Once everyone has had a turn to choose a word, the game is over and the player with the most points wins.

What Else to Play

If you love fibbing about definitions, try these board games: Dictionary Dabble, Krazy Wordz, and Balderdash. They are all based on this fun bluffing game.

Played it! ☐ Rating: ☆☆☆☆☆

Date: ___/___/_____

With: _____

Notes: _____

_____

Did You Know?

The longest word in an English language dictionary is *pneumonoultramicroscopicsilicovolcanoconiosis*. Can you guess what it means?

GAME NO.

4

Picture Consequences

AGE
LEVEL:
5 and up

Think you know your friends? Try to guess what they will draw as you work together to build an imaginary creature. The only winners of this game are the people who get to hang the finished pieces of art on their walls.

NUMBER OF PLAYERS:
3

How to Play

1. Begin by folding a piece of paper into thirds to divide up the space. Have the first player draw the head and neck of an imaginary creature on the top third of the paper. Everyone else must turn their backs or close their eyes so they don't see what has been drawn.

2. When finished, the first player folds the paper back so that nothing can be seen of the drawing except a little bit of the neck.

3. Without peeking, the second player then continues the drawing from the neck, drawing the shoulders, arms, and body. When finished, the second player folds back the paper again, so only the bottom third of the paper is visible.

4. The third player finishes the drawing with legs, tail, and more. Unfold the page to uncover the masterpiece!

WHAT YOU NEED:
Paper, pencils

WHERE TO PLAY:
Anywhere

Tip
If you have more than three people, create teams that take turns drawing each section of the page.

ACTIVITY LEVEL:
Minimal

THE POINT OF THE GAME:
Draw an imaginary figure as a group

What Else to Play

Instead of folding the paper, give each player 15 seconds to work on his or her portion of the drawing. Not in the mood for drawing? Consequences is the same game but with words. Players take turns writing parts of a story, leaving the last sentence unfinished for the next player to continue the story.

Played it! ☐ Rating: ☆☆☆☆☆

Date: ___/___/_____

With: _____

Notes: _____

_____

Did You Know?

Artists in the 1930s called this game The Exquisite Corpse and used it to create works of art.

GAME NO.

5

Dots and Boxes

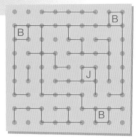

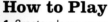

This is a simple yet addictive game that can be played on any kind of paper. All you need to do is create a square grid of dots. Leave room for multiple games—one game is almost never enough!

How to Play

1. Create a large square on graph paper, and place dots at the corners of each small square within the game board. (See sample game board above.)

2. The first player draws a line connecting two dots. The line can be vertical or horizontal but not diagonal.

3. The next player connects two more dots.

4. The first player to draw the fourth line of a box puts his or her initials in the box and gets to go again. This continues until the player draws a line that doesn't complete a box. Completing several boxes in one turn is called a "chain."

5. Once no more moves are possible, the player with the most boxes wins.

What Else to Play

Try playing Dots and Boxes but have the winner be the player who creates the fewest number of boxes. A fun alternative is to play Snake using the same grid, in which players take turns drawing a snake that cannot cross itself. The player who is forced to cross the snake loses.

Tip

Completing the first chain is not always the best strategy— this game is best played by thinking several moves ahead.

Played it! ☐ Rating: ☆☆☆☆☆

Date: ___/___/_____

With: _____

Notes: _____

_____

Five Dots

Just because this is a drawing game doesn't mean you need to be good at drawing. In fact, the more horrible the drawing, the funnier this game gets! This is an example of a non-competitive game, which means there are no winners or losers. Everyone wins because they're all laughing at the funny drawings.

How to Play

1. Each player draws five dots on a piece of paper. The dots can be scattered anywhere you want.
2. Trade your page with the other players. Using the dots as guides, draw a person. Two dots must be at the hands, two must be at the feet, and the fifth is at the head. Sound simple, right? Try it!

What Else to Play

In the game Outlines, each player draws a line on a piece of paper. The line can be squiggly, straight, zigzag, or curved. The lines are traded among the players who then must draw something incorporating the lines on the pages.

AGE LEVEL:
6 and up

NUMBER OF PLAYERS:
2 or more

WHAT YOU NEED:
Paper, pencil

Tip
Don't be afraid to draw your five-dot people in nearly impossible positions.

WHERE TO PLAY:
Anywhere

ACTIVITY LEVEL:
Minimal

THE POINT OF THE GAME:
To draw funny people with five dots as the only guide

Played it! ☐ Rating: ☆☆☆☆☆
Date: ___/___/_____
With: _____
Notes: _____
_____

GAME NO.
7

Guggenheim

Test your trivia knowledge with this classic paper and pencil game that has you delving deep into different categories.

	AUTHORS	COUNTRIES	ELEMENTS	SONGS	RELATIVES
S	SHAKESPEARE		SILICON	SUPERMAN	SUSAN SAM
T		TURKEY	TIN		
R				RUNAWAY	RICK
A	ASIMOV ANDERSEN			ANGIE	
P	POE	PERU			PAUL

How to Play

1. Each player draws a 5 x 5 game board like the one shown. As a group, choose a five-letter word, writing it vertically along the left side, one letter per row. Pick five categories, writing them across the top, one category per column.

2. Set a time limit (10 to 15 minutes). When the game starts, all players try to list as many items in each category for each letter of the word as possible. For example: If the five-letter word is STRAP, and one of the categories is countries, you could write "Turkey" under T and "Peru" under the P.

3. When time is up, each player wins one point for each unique word they come up with. If two or more players player write "Turkey," no one gets a point.

What Else to Play

Scattergories (page 126) is a fun board game version of Guggenheim.

Tip

When choosing words, avoid uncommon letters, such as X, V, Z, and Q. When choosing categories, make them broad, such as movies, TV shows, and food.

Played it! ☐ Rating: ☆☆☆☆☆
Date: ___/___/_____
With: _____
Notes: _____
_____

Mu Torere

The Maori people of New Zealand have been playing this strategy game for thousands of years. The goal of the game is to move your pieces on a star-shaped board so your opponent can no longer move. The game sounds simple, but the more you play, the more you realize the amount of strategy that's involved.

AGE LEVEL:
8 and up

NUMBER OF PLAYERS:
2

How to Play

1. Each player places four markers on one half of the game board. You can draw the board shown above on a piece of paper.

2. The player with the darker markers goes first by moving a marker to the center of the board. A marker may only move if one or both points next to it are occupied by the opponent's markers.

3. After the first move, players take turns moving onto another star point or into the center, whatever space is open. Players cannot jump over an opponent's markers.

4. The winner is the player who successfully blocks the other from making any more moves.

WHAT YOU NEED:
Paper, pencil, 4 game pieces per player (jelly beans, coins, etc.)

What Else to Play

One variation of this game is to forget about the rule that a marker may only move if one or both points next to it are occupied by the opponent's markers.

Did You Know?

In the Maori language, the game board is called the *papa takaro* and the markers are called *perepere*. The points of the star are called *kewai*, and the center point is the *putahi*.

WHERE TO PLAY:
Flat surface

Played it! ☐ Rating: ☆☆☆☆☆

Date: ___/___/_____

With: _____

Notes: _____

_____

ACTIVITY LEVEL:
Minimal

THE POINT OF THE GAME:
Block your opponent from making a move

15

GAME NO.
9

Sprouts

Challenge a friend to a game of Sprouts. All you need is a pencil, paper, and some smarts. This game is great for long car rides!

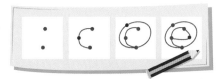

AGE LEVEL:
5 and up

NUMBER OF PLAYERS:
2

WHAT YOU NEED:
Paper, pencil

WHERE TO PLAY:
Anywhere

ACTIVITY LEVEL:
Minimal

THE POINT OF THE GAME:
To be the last player able to draw a line between two dots

How to Play

1. Draw two or more dots anywhere on a piece of paper. The more dots you start off with, the longer the game lasts.

2. The first player draws a line connecting two dots (or from one dot to itself.) Then the player adds a new dot to the midpoint of the new line.

3. The second player draws another line connecting two dots, and adds another dot to the line. The line can't cross over another line.

4. A dot with three lines connected to it is considered dead and can't have any more lines connected to it. The game ends when there are no more live dots to connect to or there's no way to connect any live dots.

What Else to Play

Brussels Sprouts is a lot like Sprouts except instead of dots you use crosses. To make a move, a player joins two free ends with a line and draws a short stroke across it. The game is over when the ends of the crosses can no longer be connected without crossing a line.

Tip

When first playing Sprouts, start with three dots. Don't add more dots until you get the hang of the game.

Did You Know?

Sprouts was invented by two British mathematicians in the 1960s.

Played it! ☐ Rating: ☆☆☆☆☆
Date: ___/___/_____
With: _____
Notes: _____
_____

Telegrams

GAME NO.

10

Telegrams allows players to create whimsical, sometimes outlandish, and often hilarious sentences based on randomly chosen letters. Who knew mnemonic devices could be so fun?

AGE LEVEL:
8 and up

How to Play

1. Make sure each player has a pencil and piece of paper. Have each player call out a letter of the alphabet until you have 10 letters. All players write these letters down in order at the top of their paper.
2. At "Go!" each player must then come up with a 10-word sentence in which each word begins with the chosen letters in consecutive order. For example, if the 10 letters are S, T, L, T, M, E, S, F, L, J, one possible sentence might read, "Sorry turtles like to make egg salad for lonely jellyfish."
3. Make things even more interesting by choosing themes for the sentences, such as: an invitation to a party, what animals say to each other, or a text from a parent to a child.

NUMBER OF PLAYERS:
3 or more

WHAT YOU NEED:
Paper, pencils

What Else to Play

Find a book of popular quotations or clichés. Have players take turns reading the first half of the quotes, while the rest of the players write down their own endings. For example: All work and no play … is what my teachers always say!

Did You Know?

A telegram was an old-fashioned way of sending a text message where an operator tapped and sent the message out in code to another operator.

WHERE TO PLAY:
Anywhere

Played it! ☐ Rating: ☆☆☆☆☆
Date: ___/___/_____
With: _____
Notes: _____
_____

ACTIVITY LEVEL:
Minimal

THE POINT OF THE GAME:
Create funny sentences

GAME NO.
11

Tic-tac-toe

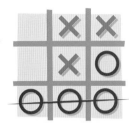

This simple game of Xs and Os can be traced all the way back to the ancient Egyptians. Even then, when played properly, Tic-tac-toe ended up in a tie.

**NUMBER
OF PLAYERS:**
2

How to Play
1. Draw a 3 x 3 grid like the one seen on the right.
2. Decide who will be "X," who will be "O," and who will go first.
3. The first player places a mark in one of the empty squares in the grid. Then the second player places a mark in an empty square.
4. Play continues until the game ends in a tie or one of the players manages to get three marks in a horizontal, vertical, or diagonal row.

Did You Know?
The ancient Romans played a version of Tic-tac-toe called *Terni Lapilli*, which means "three pebbles at a time." Each player had three pebbles, and they had to move them around to the empty places on the grid to try to get three in a row.

**WHAT YOU
NEED:**
Paper, pencil
or pen

What Else to Play
In Ghana, they play a similar game called *Achi*. Using a game board similar to the Tic-tac-toe board, each player places four markers on the points where the seven lines meet. Then they take turns moving the pieces along the lines to empty points until one player gets three markers in a row. Jumping over pieces is not allowed.

**WHERE TO
PLAY:**
Anywhere

Tip
The player who goes first has the best chance of winning.

**ACTIVITY
LEVEL:**
Minimal

**THE POINT
OF THE GAME:**
Get three of your
marks in a row

Played it! ☐ Rating: ☆☆☆☆☆
Date: ___/___/_____
With: _____
Notes: _____
_____

Beetles

This drawing game is based entirely on the luck of the roll. It doesn't matter whether or not you can draw, it's just fun to try!

AGE LEVEL:
4 and up

How to Play

1. Each player gets paper and a pencil.

2. Players take turns rolling the die. Each number on the die corresponds to a body part you can draw.

1: Draw two eyes; 2: Draw two antennae; 3: Draw six legs; 4: Draw two wings; 5: Draw one head; 6: Draw one body.

3. There are rules! You have to draw the body first, which means you can't draw anything until you roll a 6. You also have to draw a head before you can add antennae or eyes, so you have to roll a 5 before adding those.

4. The first player to finish drawing a beetle wins.

NUMBER OF PLAYERS:
2 or more

WHAT YOU NEED:
Paper, pencils, die

What Else to Play

The game Cootie is a version of this paper and pencil game that you can buy. To play, you build a 3-dimensional critter from plastic body parts.

Tip
Create your own variations of the game by drawing different creatures, aliens, monsters, and more.

WHERE TO PLAY:
Flat surface

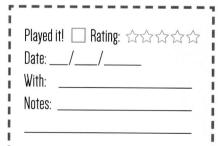

Played it! ☐ Rating: ☆☆☆☆☆
Date: ___/___/_____
With: _____
Notes: _____
_____

ACTIVITY LEVEL:
Minimal

THE POINT OF THE GAME:
Finish your beetle drawing first

GAME NO.
13

Cat's Cradle

**NUMBER
OF PLAYERS:**
2 or more

**WHAT YOU
NEED:**
36- to 40-inch
piece of string

**WHERE TO
PLAY:**
Anywhere

**ACTIVITY
LEVEL:**
Minimal

**THE POINT
OF THE GAME:**
Make shapes with
string and pass them
back and forth

Who knew you could have this much fun with a piece of string!? This game involves creating a shape with the string and then passing it to your partner and then passing it back again. How long can you keep it going without losing the shape?

How to Play

Cat's Cradle is a playground game that goes back at least 200 years. The first player makes a simple figure out of the looped string with his or her hands. This is called a cat's cradle. The second player must know exactly where to grasp the strings and how to scoop it up and into his or her own hands. This new shape is called a soldier's bed. The first player then pinches and pulls the string, ending up with yet a new shape on his or her hands, called candles. The second player, with a few more moves, then creates the manger, once again taking the strings back into his or her hands. The final shape is called the saw. If at any point the shape is lost, you both must start all over again. How fast can you complete each step without making a mistake?

What Else to Play

There are hundreds of string figures from different cultures that you can learn and incorporate into your game.

Tip

The best way to learn Cat's Cradle is to learn from someone who knows how to perform the different figures. Ask a parent or grandparent— someone will surely remember. If they don't, have a parent help you find instructions online. There are tons of videos.

Played it! ☐ Rating: ☆☆☆☆☆

Date: ___/___/_____

With: _____

Notes: _____

_____

Cup and Ball

GAME NO.

14

Children around the world have been trying to toss the ball into the cup for 700 years. It seems simple, but it takes practice.

How to Play

Cup and Ball is a traditional children's toy that consists of a small cup with a handle extending from the bottom. Attached to it is a ball on a string. The object of the game is to get the ball into the cup without touching the ball or the string. Once you get the hang of it, see how many times you can get the ball into the cup without missing. Compete against your own record or against friends.

What Else to Play

In Japan, *Kendama* ("sword" and "ball") is extremely popular. The *ken* has three cups and a spike that fits into the hole in the ball. There are many different "moves" to make with this toy, including tossing the ball into one of the three cups, catching the ball on the spike, juggling the ball between two cups, catching the ken with the dama, and many more. There are Kendama competitions held throughout the world.

Did You Know?

This game is known as *Boliche* in Spain, *Bolero* in much of Central and South America, and *Bilboquet* in France.

AGE LEVEL:
5 and up

NUMBER OF PLAYERS:
1 or more

WHAT YOU NEED:
Cup and Ball toy

WHERE TO PLAY:
Anywhere

ACTIVITY LEVEL:
Minimal

THE POINT OF THE GAME:
Catch the ball in the cup

Played it! ☐ Rating: ☆☆☆☆☆

Date: ___/___/_____

With: _____

Notes: _____

_____

GAME NO.
15

Pick-up Sticks

NUMBER OF PLAYERS:
2 or more

WHAT YOU NEED:
A bundle of 20 to 50 sticks

WHERE TO PLAY:
Flat surface

ACTIVITY LEVEL:
Light

THE POINT OF THE GAME:
Pick up the most sticks

This is a game of skill and dexterity and, well…chance! How many sticks can you pick up without disturbing any others? It all depends on how the sticks fall, and how skilled you are at picking them up again!

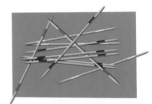

How to Play

1. Hold the bundle of sticks in one hand vertically, a few inches off the floor.
2. Drop the sticks on the ground. When all the sticks have stopped moving, you're ready to play!
3. The first player tries to pick up a stick without touching or moving any other sticks. If you pick up a stick, you can go again and try to pick up another one.
4. If you can't get a stick, or you move or touch another stick, your turn is over and play moves to the next player.
5. The person who ends up with the most sticks wins!

What Else to Play

Try playing Jacks (page 35) or Five Stones (page 30).

Did You Know?

This game is thought to have originated in ancient China, where it was called *Mikado*. The game has been played all over the world and is also known as Jack Straws or Spillikins.

Tip

You can use bamboo sticks or straws if you don't have wooden or plastic sticks!

Played it! ☐ Rating: ☆☆☆☆☆
Date: ___/___/_____
With: _____
Notes: _____
_____

20 Questions

Can you read someone else's mind? You can try with the game of 20 Questions. Try to guess what someone is thinking in 20 questions or less!

How to Play

1. The first player thinks of an object, and then tells the rest of the players the category. If the mystery word is "rabbit," the first player tells the other players it's an animal.

2. The rest of the players take turns asking questions that can only be answered with "yes" or "no." For example, "Does this animal have fur?" is a good question, but you couldn't ask "Does this animal have fur or feathers?"

3. After each question, the player who asked gets a chance to guess the mystery word. If that player guesses correctly, they win the game!

4. After 20 questions, if no one has guessed the word, the first player wins.

What Else to Play

Another fun question-and-answer game is I Spy (page 38).

Did You Know?

A version of this game is featured in "The Christmas Carol" by Charles Dickens, which was written in 1843. Games like 20 Questions were called "parlor games" and were very popular in the Victorian era.

AGE LEVEL:
3 and up

NUMBER OF PLAYERS:
3 or more

WHAT YOU NEED:
People

WHERE TO PLAY:
Anywhere

ACTIVITY LEVEL:
Minimal

THE POINT OF THE GAME:
Guess the mystery word correctly

Played it! ☐ Rating: ☆☆☆☆☆
Date: ___/___/_____
With: _____
Notes: _____
_____

GAME NO.

17

Paper Football

You can play football in the house without breaking anything—Paper Football, that is. In this simplified tabletop version of the classic sport, each player tries to get the paper football to the edge of their opponent's side of the table. No tackling necessary!

How to Play

1. To make a paper football, fold an 8 ½" x 11" (215.9 x 279.4 mm) piece of paper in half long ways, and then fold it again. Fold a top corner down to meet the side, making a triangle. Keep folding it, making triangles until you reach the bottom. Tuck the extra paper at the bottom into the pocket that was formed by all of the folding.

2. Sit opposite your opponent at a table. Start the game by placing the football flat on the table, hanging over the edge, and flick it toward the other side of the table.

3. You have four chances to make a "touchdown," or flick the football so it's hanging off your opponent's edge of the table without it falling off. If the football doesn't reach the other side, the other player gets to flick it back toward your edge of the table. If at any time the football falls off the table, the other person kicks off. Each touchdown is worth six points.

Tip
It's against the rules to push the football across the table. Only flicking, tapping, and hitting are allowed.

4. If you make a touchdown, you then kick for an extra point. Your opponent makes a finger field goal while you hold the football between your finger and thumb of your non-dominant hand, and then flick it with your index finger. If it sails through the goalposts, you earn an extra point.
5. The first player to score over 50 points wins.

What Else to Play

For added fun, add obstacles (salt shakers, napkin rings, cups, plates, and more) that you must maneuver around on the table in order to score. You can also play with a wind rule, which means that during kick offs, the opposing player can blow the paper football backward.

Played it! ☐ Rating: ☆☆☆☆☆
Date: ___/___/_____
With: _____
Notes: _____
_____

Did You Know?
Paper Football, also known as Flick Football and Finger Football, was created in 1966 by a group of elementary school boys.

GAME NO.

18

Nim

This game gets its name from the German word *nimm*, which means "take." The game is traditionally played with rows of matches, but you can use stones, spoons, bottle caps, pencils, or anything else you have a lot of.

How to Play

1. Set up your items in rows as shown.

2. Decide who goes first and alternate taking as many of the items you want from one of the rows.

3. The player forced to pick up the last item loses. Seems simple, but there is a lot of strategy involved.

What Else to Play

The African game *Tiouk-Tiouk* can be played with a checkerboard and eight checker pieces for each player. Place your pieces wherever you want on your side of the board, making sure to have one piece in each column. Take turns moving your pieces up the columns. Once opposing pieces are next to each other in a column, they are blocked and can no longer move. The last player able to make a legal move wins the game.

Did You Know?
If played correctly, the person who goes second can always win a game of Nim. Can you figure out how?

Tip
To mix things up, play with more items in each row.

Played it! ☐ Rating: ☆☆☆☆☆

Date: ___/___/_____

With: _____

Notes: _____

_____

Hot Potato

This is a great game to play at parties, especially one with a lot of guests. The more the merrier!

How to Play

1. Get in a circle, and put one person (not in the circle) in charge of the music.

2. When the music starts, start passing the "potato" to the person on the right. No throwing or skipping a person!

3. When the person in charge of the music turns the music off, the person holding the "potato" is out of the game. You can also play it so if a person drops the potato, he or she is automatically out.

4 The game continues until only one person is left.

What Else to Play

Pass the Parcel has the same rules as Hot Potato but instead of a ball, you pass around a small gift wrapped in several layers of paper. The person holding the parcel when the music stops gets to unwrap one layer. The person who unwraps the final layer gets to keep the gift.

Did You Know?

A "hot potato" is a situation or topic that no one wants to deal with. To drop something "like a hot potato" is a term that dates back to the mid-1800s. It means to abandon something very quickly.

AGE LEVEL:
7 and up

NUMBER OF PLAYERS:
4 or more

WHAT YOU NEED:
Beanbag, ball, potato, or other small item; music

WHERE TO PLAY:
Anywhere

ACTIVITY LEVEL:
Light

THE POINT OF THE GAME:
Don't get stuck holding the "hot potato"

Played it! ☐ Rating: ☆☆☆☆☆

Date: ___/___/_____

With: _____

Notes: _____

_____

GAME NO.

20

Duck, Duck, Goose

Ducks can stay put, but geese had better know how to run! In this game, if you're it, you get to tag someone as a goose, and then make a run for their spot in the circle!

How to Play

1. All the players sit in a circle, and one person is chosen to be it.

2. If you are it, walk around the outside of the circle and tap each player lightly on the head and say "duck."

3. At any time, you can decide to tap someone as the goose and run away!

4. The goose chases after and tries to tag you before you can steal the goose's seat.

5. If the goose tags you, go another round. But if you steal the goose's seat, the goose is now it.

6. Keep playing until everyone has had a chance to be both the goose and it.

What Else to Play

Fox and Hounds is another fun tag game that's also a bit like Hide and Seek. One player is chosen to be the fox, and the other players are the hounds. The fox gets a head start to run and hide, and after a set amount of time, the hounds try to find the fox!

Played it! ☐ Rating: ☆☆☆☆☆

Date: ___/___/_____

With: _____

Notes: _____

_____

Did You Know?
This game is also known as Duck, Duck, Gray Duck.

GAME NO.
21

Five Stones

AGE LEVEL:
5 and up

NUMBER OF PLAYERS:
1 or more

WHAT YOU NEED:
5 small stones

WHERE TO PLAY:
Flat surface

ACTIVITY LEVEL:
Light

THE POINT OF THE GAME:
Complete all rounds before your opponent

Similar to Jacks, this ancient game of skill will have you flipping and catching stones! There are several different steps to follow to play the game, and the player to complete all steps first wins.

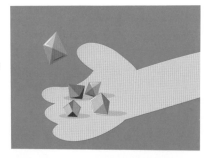

How to Play

1. Place your five stones on the ground.
2. Throw one stone up in the air, then quickly pick up another stone before you catch the one you threw. Keep going until all five stones are in your hand.
3. For round two, you have to pick up two stones at a time. For the third round, three stones, then four stones in round four.
4. For round five, throw one stone in the air and place four stones on the ground. Toss the same stone again, then pick up all four stones.
5. Finally, throw all five stones up in the air and try to catch them on the back of your hand.

What Else to Play

Try creating your own steps to follow each round. For example, pick up two stones, throw one in the air, and quickly exchange the stone in your hand with one on the ground.

Did You Know?

Five Stones is also a well-known game in Korea, where it's called *Kongki Noli*.

Played it! ☐ Rating: ☆☆☆☆☆
Date: ___/___/_____
With: _____
Notes: _____
_____

30

Hot and Cold

In this game, if you're feeling the heat, it means you're close to the jackpot! You can play this one anywhere at any time—and it sure makes looking for something so much more fun!

How to Play

1. Choose an object to hide, and have the other players close their eyes as you hide the object from them.

3. As the other players start searching for the hidden object, let them know if they're getting "hot" (moving closer to the hiding spot) or "cold" (moving farther from the hiding spot.)

4. If they're "getting warmer," they're getting closer. Make it fun by comparing the distance to things that are hot or cold, such as "You're getting hotter like a pizza oven!" or "You're getting colder like the North Pole!"

5. As they close in on the hiding spot, be sure to let them know they are getting hotter and hotter until they find it!

What Else to Play

The Floor is Lava is just what it sounds like—and your goal is to not melt! One player is it and all the other players pretend the ground is lava. If you touch it, you melt! It is the only one allowed on the ground, and runs around trying to tag the other players to be out.

Played it! ☐ Rating: ☆☆☆☆☆
Date: ___/___/_____
With: _____
Notes: _____
_____

AGE LEVEL:
3 and up

NUMBER OF PLAYERS:
2 or more

WHAT YOU NEED:
Small object to hide

WHERE TO PLAY:
Anywhere

ACTIVITY LEVEL:
Light

THE POINT OF THE GAME:
Find the hidden object

GAME NO.

23

Musical Chairs

AGE LEVEL:
3 and up

NUMBER OF PLAYERS:
4 or more

WHAT YOU NEED:
Music, chairs, someone to play and stop the music

WHERE TO PLAY:
Large room or outdoor area

ACTIVITY LEVEL:
Moderate

THE POINT OF THE GAME:
Grab a seat when the music ends

Perfect for a rainy day, family game night, or a birthday party, Musical Chairs will have everyone movin' and groovin' and lookin' for a chair to steal!

How to Play

1. Place the chairs in two rows with their backs touching. There should be one less chair than the number of players.

2. Start the music! While the music is playing, the players walk (or dance!) around the chairs, moving in a circle.

3. When the music stops, everyone must race to sit in a chair.

4. Whoever doesn't get a chair is out!

5. Take one chair away and start the next round. Keep playing until there's just one person left sitting—the winner!

What Else to Play

No chairs? That's okay, you can play this game on the ground. When the music stops, sit on the floor as fast as you can. The last to sit is out!

Did You Know?

"Musical chairs" is something people say to describe a particularly confusing or quickly changing series of events.

Played it! ☐ Rating: ☆☆☆☆☆

Date: ___/___/_____

With: _____

Notes: _____

_____

32

Simon Says

How well can you listen and follow directions? Simon Says tests your concentration and is a super-fun game to play with your friends— especially if the Simon has a good sense of humor!

AGE LEVEL:
3 and up

NUMBER OF PLAYERS:
4 or more

How to Play
1. Choose who will be Simon.
2. Simon tells the players what to do by saying "Simon says…" and then a command. It could be as simple as "Simon says raise your right hand" or as silly as "Simon says cross your eyes." Everyone has to do what Simon says!
3. If Simon doesn't say "Simon says" before a command, don't move!
4. Anyone who moves when they're not supposed to is out. The last player standing gets to be Simon in the next round!

What Else to Play
Try out Red Light, Green Light (page 75) and Mother May I (page 69) next!

Tip
Get creative with your commands! Here are some fun ideas to get you started: Simon says: Tickle your feet, make a funny face, fly like a superhero, sing your favorite song, break dance.

WHAT YOU NEED:
People

WHERE TO PLAY:
Large room or outdoor area

ACTIVITY LEVEL:
Light to moderate

Played it! ☐ Rating: ☆☆☆☆☆
Date: ___/___/_____
With: _____
Notes: _____
_____

THE POINT OF THE GAME:
Listen and do what Simon says

33

GAME NO.
25

Beanbag Toss

AGE LEVEL:
8 and up

NUMBER OF PLAYERS:
2 or more

WHAT YOU NEED:
Sidewalk chalk
Beanbag for each player

WHERE TO PLAY:
Large room or outdoor area

ACTIVITY LEVEL:
Light

THE POINT OF THE GAME:
Score the most points

This game is un-bean-lievably fun! Hit the target with your beanbag and get points. The player with the best aim wins the game!

How to Play

1. Draw a big target on the sidewalk with chalk at least 2 feet (.6 meters) wide. You can make it look like a bullseye, or slice it up like a pie.
2. Assign a different number to each space inside the target.
3. Draw a throwing line about 8 feet (2.5 meters) back from the target.
4. Stand behind the throwing line and take turns tossing the beanbags at the target.
5. Try different throws. Maybe an underhand toss will get you closer than an overhand throw!
6. The number in the space you land on is the amount of points you get.

What Else to Play

Want to make it harder? Use a blindfold! How many points can you get without seeing where you're throwing?

Tip

You can make your own beanbags! Just fill the toe of an old sock with some dried beans and tie the top off.

Played it! ☐ Rating: ☆☆☆☆☆

Date: ___/___/_____

With: _____

Notes: _____

_____

Jacks

Children all over the world play this game, although some call it another name—sometimes Jackstones or Dibs. Wherever you play, the rules are simple, and you can play by yourself or with a group of friends, which makes it fun to play anywhere!

How to Play

1. Place all the jacks on a smooth surface in front of you.

2. Throw the ball up in the air, and pick up one of the jacks. Let the ball bounce once, then catch it with the same hand.

3. If you catch it, go on to the next round, and try to pick up two jacks this time.

4. Keep going, with three jacks, and then four, until you can pick up all the jacks. If you miss, it's the next player's turn.

What Else to Play

Once you've mastered Jacks, try Eggs in the Basket! Move the jack(s) you pick up to your free hand before you catch the ball. You've got to be quick!

> ## Tip
> It's best to play on a hard surface, like wood or concrete, so the ball can bounce.

Played it! ☐ Rating: ☆☆☆☆☆
Date: ___/___/_____
With: _____
Notes: _____
_____

AGE LEVEL:
6 and up

NUMBER OF PLAYERS:
1 or more

WHAT YOU NEED:
5 jacks, small bouncy ball

WHERE TO PLAY:
Flat surface

ACTIVITY LEVEL:
Light

THE POINT OF THE GAME:
To pick up all the jacks

GAME NO.

27

Limbo

AGE
LEVEL:
6 and up

How low can you go? Test your flexibility and balance with this popular game! The lower the stick goes, the lower you'll have to go. This is a great game to play with some friends on a sunny day outside. Put some fun music on, pick a shady spot, and let's limbo!

How to Play

1. Choose two players to hold the stick. To start, hold the stick about chest-level.

NUMBER
OF PLAYERS:
1 or more

2. All other players line up behind the stick.

3. One at a time, each player must go under the stick, bending backward if necessary.

4. If you touch the stick, you're out! You can't touch the ground either (other than your feet).

5. Once everyone in line has gone through, lower the stick a few inches for everyone to go through again. Each time gets tougher!

6. Keep lowering the stick and going through the line until there is just one person left who can go under it.

WHAT YOU
NEED:
A broom or other
stick or pole

What Else to Play

Try backward Limbo or sideways Limbo! Walk backward leading up to the stick, or try to go under sideways. Even more fun? Limbo on roller skates!

WHERE TO
PLAY:
Large room or
outdoor area

ACTIVITY
LEVEL:
Moderate

THE POINT
OF THE GAME:
To go as low as you can

Played it! ☐ Rating: ☆☆☆☆☆

Date: ___/___/_____

With: _____

Notes: _____

_____

Did You Know?

The Limbo started as a dance contest in the West Indies, on the island of Trinidad. It became popular in the US in the 1950s, and even more so when the song "Limbo Rock" by Chubby Checker became a big hit in 1962.

GAME NO.
28

I Spy

AGE
LEVEL:
4 and up

If you like detective work, then this is the game for you! All you need is a keen eye and the ability to notice details to solve this mystery. It's perfect for road trips, rainy days, and any other time you need to add a little fun to your day.

NUMBER
OF PLAYERS:
2 or more

How to Play
1. The first player gets to be the spy.
2. The spy looks around the area and chooses one object without telling anyone. Everyone has to be able to see this object.
3. The spy then gives a clue to the other players by saying, "I spy with my little eye, something that ..." You can say "...something that starts with the letter B." or "...something that a person needs to open every day."
4. Each player gets a chance to guess. If no one gets it, the spy can give another hint.
5. Whoever guesses correctly is the next spy!

WHAT YOU
NEED:
People

What Else to Play
If you like question-and-answer games like this one, try playing 20 Questions (page 23)!

WHERE TO
PLAY:
Anywhere

Tip
For a challenge, try choosing sounds, such as falling rain or an overhead plane, instead of objects.

ACTIVITY
LEVEL:
Minimal

**THE POINT
OF THE GAME:**
Guess the correct
object

Played it! ☐ Rating: ☆☆☆☆☆

Date: ___ / ___ / _____

With: _____

Notes: _____

_____

Tip

Be sure to avoid looking at the object when making your announcement.

GAME NO.

29

Twister

How flexible are you? The game of Twister can get pretty twisted. It all depends on where the spinner lands, and how bendy you can be!

NUMBER OF PLAYERS:
2 to 4

How to Play

1. Players take their places on the mat, and the referee spins the spinner, calling out where it lands (a color and a body part). For example, "right hand, yellow."

2. Each player must follow the direction and place the designated body part on a free circle of that color.

3. If your called-out hand or foot is already on that color, you have to place it on a different free circle of that color.

4. If two players reach for the same circle at the same time, the referee decides who gets it.

5. If you fall or touch the mat with your elbow or knee, you're out! The last one standing (or twisting!) is the winner.

WHAT YOU NEED:
Twister mat, spinner, referee

Did You Know?
The world record for the largest game of Twister used more than 1,200 Twister mats!

WHERE TO PLAY:
Large room or outdoor area

What Else to Play

For another body-bending game, check out Limbo (page 36)!

ACTIVITY LEVEL:
Light to moderate

THE POINT OF THE GAME:
Twist up the other players

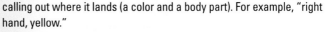

Played it! ☐ Rating: ☆☆☆☆☆

Date: ___/___/_____

With: _____

Notes: _____

_____

Statues

Strike a pose—and stay that way! Staying as still as a statue is only half the battle. You have to be able to move quickly too!

How to Play

1. Choose a player to be it.

2. It stands at one end of the yard at the finish line with his or her back to the other players.

3. It calls out "ready, set, go" and then counts (slow or fast) to 5. All players run forward and try to tag it.

4. At the count of five, it turns back around and the rest of the players must freeze into statues.

5. Anyone still moving when it turns around must go back to the starting line.

6. Play continues until it is tagged, and then it has to chase the players and try to tag one of them back. If someone else gets tagged, he or she is it and everyone goes back to the starting line to play again!

What Else to Play

Play Musical Statues by turning the music on and asking everyone to dance. As soon as the music stops, everyone must freeze into a statue! For extra fun, the person controlling the music can also yell out what kind of statue they want the players to be, like animals or famous people.

Played it! ☐ Rating: ☆☆☆☆☆

Date: ___/___/_____

With: _____

Notes: _____

_____

AGE LEVEL:
5 and up

NUMBER OF PLAYERS:
3 or more

WHAT YOU NEED:
A starting line and a finish line

WHERE TO PLAY:
Large outdoor area

ACTIVITY LEVEL:
Moderate

THE POINT OF THE GAME:
Tag it while making cool statue poses

41

GAME NO.

31

Hide and Seek

AGE LEVEL:
3 and up

You can play Hide and Seek at home, on a busy playground with lots of equipment, in a field with lots of hiding places, or in any safe area where there are enough hiding places for everyone who wants to play.

How to Play

1. Choose a home base and select the first player to be the seeker.

NUMBER OF PLAYERS:
3 or more

2. The seeker stands at home base, covers his or her eyes, and counts to 50 (or 100 for larger play areas). The rest of the players run away and hide.

3. After counting, the seeker yells, "Ready or not, here I come!" and starts looking for the hiding players.

4. When the seeker spots a hidden player, he or she must call out that player's name, and then chase the player back to home base. If the seeker gets there first, he or she calls out "One, two, three, on (player's name)," and that player is caught. If the player gets to home base first, he or she calls out, "One, two, three, home free!" and that player is safe.

WHAT YOU NEED:
Good places to hide

5. Once all the players have been found, the first player who was caught becomes the seeker.

WHERE TO PLAY:
Large outdoor area

Tip
Make sure all the players know the boundaries of the playing area.

ACTIVITY LEVEL:
Moderate

THE POINT OF THE GAME:
Don't get found by the seeker

What Else to Play

Try playing Sardines. In this game, only one person hides. When one of the other players finds the person, that player must hide in the same spot. This gets fun as more and more people find the hiding spot and squish in with the others. The last person to find the group is the next person to hide.

Played it! ☐ Rating: ☆☆☆☆☆
Date: ___/ ___/ _____
With: _____
Notes: _____
_____

Did You Know?
There's an international hide and seek competition held every year in Consonno, Italy, which is a ghost town that features a medieval castle, dance hall, and bizarre buildings.

GAME NO.
32

Hula Hoop Race

AGE LEVEL:
5 and up

NUMBER OF PLAYERS:
8 or more

WHAT YOU NEED:
2 hula hoops

WHERE TO PLAY:
Outdoors

ACTIVITY LEVEL:
Moderate

THE POINT OF THE GAME:
Pass the hula hoop through the human chain

Hula hoops are awesome for spinning around your waist, neck, legs, and arms. They're also good for racing! This race is perfect for parties when you have a lot of people around. It's best played outdoors. (If you're careful you can try it in a large, indoor space like a gym.)

How to Play
1. Divide players into two teams. Each team lines up single-file while holding hands, creating a chain. The player at the beginning of each line holds a hula hoop.
2. At "Go!" each team works to pass the hula hoop from one end to the other without letting hands go. Players have to wiggle the hoop over their heads and lift their legs to step through the hoop.
3. The first team to get the hoop to the free hand of the player on the opposite end of the chain wins.

What Else to Play
If you have a lot of hula hoops, place them on the ground and play hopscotch with them. If you only have one hula hoop, try jumping over it like a jump rope.

Did You Know?
The modern hula hoop was invented by Spud Melin and Richard Knerr in 1958; however kids have been playing with hoops since ancient times.

Played it! ☐ Rating: ☆☆☆☆☆
Date: ___/___/_____
With: _____
Notes: _____
_____

44

Cat and
Mouse

GAME NO.
33

This outdoor game is a little bit like Duck, Duck, Goose, except faster!

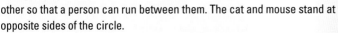

How to Play

1. Choose a mouse and a cat. Have the rest of the players form a circle standing far enough away from each other so that a person can run between them. The cat and mouse stand at opposite sides of the circle.

2. At "Go!" the cat chases the mouse around the outside of the circle. If the cat or mouse runs through one of the spaces in the circle, the two people on either side of the space close it by holding hands.

3. The game continues until all the spaces close, the cat catches the mouse, or either one is trapped inside the circle.

What Else to Play

There are lots of different ways to play this game. One variation has the players forming the circle already holding hands as the mouse weaves in and out while the cat remains on the outside trying to catch the mouse. Another variation requires both the cat and the mouse to start outside the circle, where the cat must follow the mouse's moves.

AGE LEVEL:
4 and up

NUMBER OF PLAYERS:
8 or more

WHAT YOU NEED:
People

WHERE TO PLAY:
Large outdoor area

Tip

This game is best played with many players—the more players, the larger the circle!

ACTIVITY LEVEL:
Moderate

THE POINT OF THE GAME:
Don't get caught inside the circle

Played it! ☐ Rating: ☆☆☆☆☆

Date: ___/___/_____

With: _____

Notes: _____

_____

GAME NO.

34

Capture the Flag

AGE LEVEL:
6 and up

The object of the game is to capture the other team's flag and return it to your side of the field. But don't get tagged, or you'll end up in jail!

NUMBER OF PLAYERS:
6 or more

How to Play

1. Divide the playing field down the middle with a long rope or other boundary marker. Split the players into two teams. Each team gets one side of the field, where they pick a spot for the jail and for their flag. The flag must be visible to the other team and easy to reach. You can use brightly colored bandannas or T-shirts for flags.

2. When the game begins, players sneak onto the other team's territory and try to find and capture its flag. If players are tagged, they go to jail. You can only tag someone if they are on your side of the field.

WHAT YOU NEED:
Two "flags," boundary markers

3. If you reach the other team's flag, grab it and run back to your side of the field. If you get tagged on the other team's side, you go to jail and the flag is returned to its original position. Players can be rescued from jail if a teammate tags them.

4. The team that successfully captures the opposing team's flag and runs it across the boundary wins!

WHERE TO PLAY:
Large outdoor area

Tip

You cannot move your flag during the game! When running with the opponent's flag, hand it off to a teammate before you get tagged.

ACTIVITY LEVEL:
Highly active

THE POINT OF THE GAME:
Capture the other team's flag

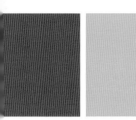

What Else to Play

If you want to create a more challenging game, give each team more than one flag and the opportunity to recapture its flag. Or let the teams hide their flags, rather than keeping them out in the open. For a fun twist, try playing at night with flashlights!

Played it! ☐ Rating: ☆☆☆☆☆

Date: ___/___/_____

With: _____

Notes: _____

_____

Did You Know?

Students at the University of Minnesota stage massive Capture the Flag tournaments on Friday nights, with more than a hundred students playing at any given time.

GAME NO.
35

Clothespins

AGE LEVEL:
5 and up

NUMBER OF PLAYERS:
2 or more

WHAT YOU NEED:
Lots of clothespins

WHERE TO PLAY:
Large outdoor area

ACTIVITY LEVEL:
Highly active

THE POINT OF THE GAME:
Catch your opponents' clothespins

Do you know what a clothespin is? If not, ask a parent. And then grab a bunch of them for this really fun tag game that has elements of flag football.

How to Play

1. Have players pin five clothespins anywhere to their clothing (shirts, sleeves, pant legs, pockets). The clothespins must be visible.

2. Define your playing area, and at "Go!" each player runs around trying to grab other players' clothespins. After grabbing a clothespin, you must kneel down (which means you can't be tagged) and attach it to your clothing.

3. If you lose all of your clothespins, you're out of the game. The player with all the clothespins at the end of the game or the player with the most clothespins after a predetermined time (10 minutes or so) is the winner.

What Else to Play

Play in a small, circled off area so that you can duck and dive, but can't run too far. Also check out different versions of Tag (page 84).

Tip

If a player kneels without first grabbing a new clothespin, they have to give a clothespin to the player nearest to them.

Played it! ☐ Rating: ☆☆☆☆☆

Date: ___/___/_____

With: _____

Notes: _____

_____

48

Pitching Pennies

All you need for this game is a pocketful of change and a wall. Pockets empty? Try playing the game with different items, such as playing cards, stones, rolled-up socks, marbles, and whatever else you have at hand.

How to Play

1. Have each player stand 10 to 15 feet (1.5 to 3 meters) from the wall and take turns throwing a coin at it.

2. The player with the coin closest to the wall wins the round and gets a point.

3. The player with the most points after 10 rounds wins the game.

4. If there is a tie, with two coins equally close to the wall, no points are awarded for the round. If a coin lands on top of the closest coin, the top coin gets the point.

5. If you have enough coins, give each player 10 coins. After each round, the winner collects the losing coins from the ground. The player with the most coins after 10 rounds wins. Once a player loses all their coins, they are out until the next game.

What Else to Play

If playing with cards, place a baseball cap by the wall and try to flick cards into or near the hat.

Did You Know?

Pitching Pennies is an ancient game that usually involved winners keeping the coins.

Played it! ☐ Rating: ☆☆☆☆☆

Date: ___/___/_____

With: _____

Notes: _____

_____

AGE LEVEL:
6 and up

NUMBER OF PLAYERS:
2 or more

WHAT YOU NEED:
Coins for each player

WHERE TO PLAY:
Near a wall

ACTIVITY LEVEL:
Light

THE POINT OF THE GAME:
Toss your coin closest to the wall

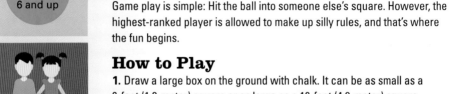

Outdoor Game

GAME NO.
37

Four Square

AGE LEVEL:
6 and up

NUMBER OF PLAYERS:
4 or more

WHAT YOU NEED:
Rubber ball, chalk

WHERE TO PLAY:
Playground or driveway

ACTIVITY LEVEL:
Moderate

THE POINT OF THE GAME:
Eliminate the other players to achieve the highest rank

This game has a lot of different rules depending on where you play it. Game play is simple: Hit the ball into someone else's square. However, the highest-ranked player is allowed to make up silly rules, and that's where the fun begins.

How to Play

1. Draw a large box on the ground with chalk. It can be as small as a 6-foot (1.8-meter) square or as large as a 16-foot (4.9-meter) square. Divide this box into four squares. Label the boxes Ace, King, Queen, and Jack.

2. Have four players stand in or near the boxes.

3. Play begins with the Ace bouncing the ball in his or her box and then into another player's box. The next player must then hit the ball into someone else's box, and so on. The Ace always serves.

4. If the ball doesn't land in another box, hits one of the inside lines, bounces more than once in a player's own box, or if another player catches the ball before it bounces in the next square, the player that hit the ball last is out. A ball that lands on the outside line of someone's box is considered in bounds and is still in play.

5. Once out, the player moves to the Jack position while everyone else moves up a rank. If there are more than four players, a new player becomes the Jack. Whoever is Ace at the end of the game wins … until next time.

Tip
Depending on local tradition, some special rules make it almost impossible for the Ace to ever lose his or her place. Outlaw those rules and just keep the ones that make the game more challenging for everyone. Ask other kids and your parents for Four Square rules they may know and teach them to your friends.

6. Most games of Four Square are played with special rules that the Ace gets to announce before each round. For instance, if the Ace yells, "Popcorn," players can juggle the ball between hands before hitting it. "Double Bounces" means players have to wait for the ball to bounce twice in their box before hitting it. The rules only last for one serve and the Ace has to yell new rules each time.

What Else to Play

Not enough players for Four Square? Try Two Square! Same game, but with two players. The first player to 21 points wins the game.

Played it! ☐ Rating: ☆☆☆☆☆

Date: ___/___/_____

With: _____

Notes: _____

_____

Did You Know?
Many playgrounds, basketball courts, indoor gymnasiums, and school yards have permanent Four Square courts. Keep your eyes open for one near you. The world record for longest game of Four Square is 34 hours.

GAME NO.

38

Disc Golf

AGE LEVEL:
7 and up

Disc Golf is a lot like regular golf. The goal is to get a flying disc to hit a target in the fewest number of tries. You can play on a Disc Golf course at some parks, which have baskets as targets. You can also play with several different kinds of discs. However, a regular Frisbee® and items in a park can serve as your targets just fine. A Disc Golf game usually lasts 9 or 18 holes, although you can play as many holes as you have time for.

NUMBER OF PLAYERS:
2 and up

How to Play

1. Set up your targets. Depending on how challenging you want your course to be, stand anywhere from 25 feet (7.6 meters) to 100 yards (91 meters) away from the first target.

2. Take turns throwing the flying disc at the first target. If a player hits it on the first try, they get 1 point. If a player hits the target on the second try, they get a 2 points, and so on. Keep track of the number of tries it takes to hit all the targets.

WHAT YOU NEED:
Flying disc, disc golf course (or homemade course), pencil, pad

3. When every player has hit the first target, all of the players move on to the second target. Continue to play until all the players have hit all the targets.

4. The player with the fewest points at the end of the game wins.

WHERE TO PLAY:
Large outdoor field with targets

Tip

Sometimes it's best not to try to hit a target on the first throw. Strategize the best way to reach the target without throwing your Frisbee up a tree.

ACTIVITY LEVEL:
Moderate

THE POINT OF THE GAME:
Hit targets in the fewest number of tries

What Else to Play

You can do target practice with footballs, baseballs, paper airplanes, and more! Whoever gets the most hits wins. Try this variation to make the game more interesting: Give each player a set amount of throws for the entire game. The player who gets the farthest wins.

Played it! ☐ Rating: ☆☆☆☆☆

Date: ___/___/_____

With: _____

Notes: _____

_____

Did You Know?

The first recorded game of Disc Golf took place in 1926.

GAME NO.

39

Hit the Penny

AGE LEVEL:
5 and up

NUMBER OF PLAYERS:
2

WHAT YOU NEED:
Penny, small rubber ball

WHERE TO PLAY:
On the sidewalk

ACTIVITY LEVEL:
Light

THE POINT OF THE GAME:
Hit the penny with the ball

Hit the Penny is one of those games your parents or grandparents will remember playing—especially if they lived in a big city. Like many cities around the world, New York in the 1950s had a lot of people but not a lot of space. That didn't stop kids from playing fun games though. This game, along with many others (including several in this book) were invented by New York's children and are still played today. All you need to play is a hard surface with some sort of crack in it. And for a fun twist, play with an ice-pop stick instead of a coin.

How to Play

1. Find a sidewalk with squares.
2. Place a coin on the line between two squares.
3. Have each player stand on the far end of each sidewalk square. (If you're playing on unmarked concrete, make sure players are the same distance away from the coin.)
4. Take turns trying to hit the coin with the ball. You get one point for hitting the coin and two points for flipping it.
5. The first player to reach 21 points wins the game.

Tip

If the other player hits the penny into your square, it's now closer to you and easier to score. Try hitting the coin softly with the ball so it won't flip back over to the other player's side.

What Else to Play

In Brazil, Chile, and other South American countries, Hit the Coin is a very different game. To play, firmly stick a thick 12- to 18-inch (30- to 36-centimeter) dowel or stick into the ground. (You play this game on dirt.) Draw a 5-inch-diameter (13-centimeter) circle around the stick, then balance a coin on top of the stick. Have all the players stand about 4 feet (1.2 centimeters) away and take turns trying to knock the coin off the stick by throwing another coin at it. The object is to knock the coin off the stick and outside of the 5-inch (13-centimeter) circle. The first player to reach 21 points wins.

Played it! ☐ Rating: ☆☆☆☆☆

Date: ___/___/_____

With: _____

Notes: _____

_____

Did You Know?

The ball of choice for street games was the Spalding® High-Bounce Ball, which kids called a Spaldeen. It is a pink rubber ball, sort of like a tennis ball without the felt. Today, you can buy Spaldeens in many different colors.

Hopscotch

This ancient hopping game has been played by children for hundreds of years just about everywhere around the world.

How to Play

1. Draw the hopscotch course with chalk on a sidewalk or in the dirt, and give each player a small stone, called a marker.

2. Take turns tossing your markers into the first box without it touching any lines or bouncing out. If either happens, your turn is over.

3. Hop through the hopscotch course, turn around in the safe zone, and hop back. On the way back, pick up the marker. Then toss your marker into the second box and repeat the process. If, while hopping through the course, you step on a line, miss a box, or fall, your turn ends. As for how to hop through the course, any row with one box (1, 2, 3, 6, and 9) must be hopped into on one foot. Rows with 4, 5 and 7, 8 can be jumped into with one foot landing in one box and the other foot landing in the other.

4. Older kids may want to play where the box with their marker in it must be hopped over and skipped. If you land in the box that has your marker in it, you lose your turn.

5. The first player to complete the course for every number wins.

NUMBER OF PLAYERS:
2 or more

WHAT YOU NEED:
Chalk,
Small stones

WHERE TO PLAY:
On the sidewalk, dirt field, or just about anywhere outside

Tip

Make the Hopscotch course more challenging by changing the shape, adding more boxes, or making boxes that can't be landed on.

ACTIVITY LEVEL:
Light

THE POINT OF THE GAME:
Navigate the hopscotch course

What Else to Play

Various versions are played around the world. Try these:

• Call out various items in a category (colors, flowers, types of cars) while hopping through the court. If you can't name anything, you're out.

• Complete the course in 30 seconds (or another time limit).

• Instead of throwing the markers in numerical order, toss them into any box. After completing a turn, initial the square where your marker landed. The person with the most initialed boxes wins.

• Kick your marker from space to space with your hopping foot as you jump through the course.

Played it! ☐ Rating: ☆☆☆☆☆

Date: ___/___/_____

With: _____

Notes: _____

_____

Did You Know?

Hopscotch began in ancient Britain during the early Roman Empire. The original Hopscotch courts were 100 feet (30.5 meters) long and used for military training. Roman soldiers ran and hopped the course wearing full armor and carrying heavy loads.

Handball

THE POINT
OF THE GAME:
Score the most points
by successfully hitting
the ball

Handball courts are in city playgrounds and recreation centers, but you can play anywhere there's an open wall—even against a garage door.

How to Play

1. Create a serving line and out of bounds area. An official court is 20 feet by 34 feet (6.1 meters by 10.4 meters) with a serving line 16 feet (4.9 meters) from the wall, but your court can be as big or small as you want it to be.

2. Stand behind the serving line and serve the ball by bouncing it on the ground once and hitting it against the wall with an open palm. The ball must bounce off the wall and back over the serving line to begin play. The server gets two tries. If both serves fail, the opponent takes over the serve.

3. Once the ball is in play, the opposing player must hit it back against the wall with an open palm before the ball bounces a second time. The players take turns hitting the ball against the wall. Only the serve has to pass the serving line.

4. If the server loses the volley, the other player gets a point and gets to serve. If the opponent loses the volley, the server gets the point. The first player to get 21 points wins.

What Else to Play

Hand Tennis is played on a tennis court. Teams bat a ball back and forth over the net as if your hands were rackets.

Tip

When playing in smaller areas, control how hard you hit the ball.

Played it! ☐ Rating: ☆☆☆☆☆

Date: ___/___/_____

With: _____

Notes: _____

_____

Jump Rope

For Jump Rope, all you need is a rope. There are a bunch of rhymes and songs you can jump to by yourself and be perfectly happy; however, there are also some fun games to play with others to make it even more interesting.

How to Play

1. Two players each take one end of the rope and start to turn it, making sure to stand close enough together so the top of the jump rope is higher than the jumper's head.

2. The jumper jumps into the middle of the jump rope, and players count out how many times the jumper makes it successfully over the turning rope. When the jumper gets tangled up in the rope, it's someone else's turn.

What Else to Play

For Double Dutch, turn two jump ropes in different directions! (This takes some practice.) Or try a game of Helicopter: one player grabs one rope handle, bends down, and swings the rope in a circle, acting like a helicopter. The rope must remain as close to the ground as possible, and the players have to keep jumping over the helicopter rope. Anyone who gets tangled in the rope is out.

AGE LEVEL:
7 and up

NUMBER OF PLAYERS:
3 or more

WHAT YOU NEED:
At least one jump rope

WHERE TO PLAY:
Outdoors

ACTIVITY LEVEL:
Moderate to highly active

THE POINT OF THE GAME:
See how long you can jump

Played it! ☐ Rating: ☆☆☆☆☆
Date: ___ / ___ / _____
With: _____
Notes: _____
_____

GAME NO.

43

Steal the Bacon

AGE LEVEL:
5 and up

NUMBER OF PLAYERS:
3 or more

WHAT YOU NEED:
Cap, water bottle, or other item to serve as the "bacon"

WHERE TO PLAY:
Large outdoor area

ACTIVITY LEVEL:
Highly active

THE POINT OF THE GAME:
Bring home the bacon safely

It's not money—and it's definitely not a pig! The bacon in this game is actually a cap, water bottle, or anything else you can easily grab.

How to Play

1. Pick a referee for the round. Mark off two lines on opposite sides of a field—anywhere from 30 to 50 feet (9.1 to 15.2 meters) apart. Place the "bacon" in the middle of the field.

2. Divide players into two teams and count off so each player on the team has a number. The teams line up behind the lines on opposite sides of the field.

3. When the referee calls out a number, the player from each team with that number rushes toward the bacon.

4. The player who reaches the bacon first grabs it and tries to run back before the other player can tag him or her. If the bacon-grabber crosses the line safely, he or she wins a point for the team. If bacon-grabber is tagged, the other team gets a point.

5. Once the referee has called every number, the team with the most points is the winner.

What Else to Play

For a fun variation, have the referee call out more than one number at the same time. Or give the referee the ability to yell, "Steal the bacon!" in which all the players run for the bacon at the same time.

Tip

If you have a large enough group, create a square playing area with four teams instead of two.

GAME NO.

44

Kick the Can

This is the perfect outdoor game. All you need is an old cola can and an outdoor play area with places to hide. You can play with as few as three people or as many as twenty. The game requires speed, strategy, and cunning, and you can play for hours and never get tired of it.

How to Play

1. Set up the boundaries of the playing area, and decide where the can and the "jail" for caught players will be located. (The can should be clearly visible in the center of the playing area.) Choose the first seeker.

2. The seeker counts to 100 (or whatever number you choose) with closed eyes while the rest of the players run to find hiding spots. When finished counting, the seeker begins searching for the hiding players.

3. After finding someone, the seeker calls out the player's name and hiding place. At that moment, both the hider and the seeker race to the can. If the seeker kicks the can first, the hider has to go to jail. If the hider kicks the can first, all jailed players are freed and the game is reset, and the hiders can find new hiding spots.

4. At any time, a hider can run to kick the can to free anyone who is in jail. However, if the seeker gets to the can first, that hider is jailed.

5. The game is over when the seeker has successfully jailed all the players, or everyone is called in for dinner. The last hider is the new seeker.

Tip

Place small stones inside the can so it makes lots of noise when kicked. Also, put a time limit on how long players have to be seekers. Fifteen to thirty minutes is long enough.

What Else to Play

Kick the Can is similar to hide-and-seek games (page 42), Capture the Flag (page 46), and Tag (page 84), so if you like this game, try those next!

Played it! ☐ Rating: ☆☆☆☆☆

Date: ___/___/_____

With: _____

Notes: _____

_____

Did You Know?

Kick the Can became a popular game in the United States during the Great Depression in the 1930s because kids could play the game anywhere and only needed an old tin can to play.

GAME NO.

45

Kickball

This simplified baseball game uses feet instead of bats and a dodgeball instead of a baseball.

How to Play

1. Set up the bases like a baseball diamond. The bases should be around 25 feet (7.6 meters) apart with the pitcher's mound in the middle, but closer to home plate.

2. Divide the players into two equal teams, and decide which team will bat first while the other team takes the field.

3. The pitcher rolls the ball to the first player. The kicker has three chances to kick the ball before getting an out.

4. After kicking the ball in fair territory (inside the foul lines), the fielders try to get the kicker out. To record an out, a fielder can catch the ball in the air for an automatic out, throw the ball to a base before the kicker gets there, tag the kicker off-base, or hit the kicker below the waist with the ball.

5. Once safely at one of the bases, the kicker waits until the next player on their team kicks the ball. Then the baserunners circle the bases, trying to make it to home plate safely. A baserunner needs to remain on their base if a ball is caught on a fly.

6. After three outs, the two teams switch roles. The team with the most runs after seven full turns (called innings) wins.

Tip

Instead of playing to three outs, have each half inning last only until each player has had one chance to kick. The half inning then ends (no matter who is left on base) and teams switch roles. This is a great way for young players to experience the game.

What Else to Play

Try out another variation of baseball! Instead of a bat or a kickball, use a small, bouncy ball and your hand as a bat.

Played it! ☐ Rating: ☆☆☆☆☆

Date: ___/___/_____

With: _____

Notes: _____

_____

Did You Know?

Kick Baseball was invented in 1917 by Nicholas C. Seuss, and the game was used to teach children the fundamentals of baseball. Kickball is popular in South Korea, where it is called *Balyagu*.

GAME NO.
46

Marbles

AGE LEVEL:
6 and up

NUMBER OF PLAYERS:
2 or more

WHAT YOU NEED:
Marbles, chalk

WHERE TO PLAY:
Outdoors on a flat surface

ACTIVITY LEVEL:
Light

THE POINT OF THE GAME:
Knock the marbles out of the circle

There's something almost magical about those little glass or clay balls. Even if you have never played a game of marbles in your life, you can probably find a few in your home. Archaeologists have found evidence throughout the world of marble games dating back thousands of years. The funny thing about marbles is that there isn't one set of rules; there are hundreds of different marbles games to play. Here is a basic game along with a couple of variations.

How to Play

1. With a piece of chalk, draw a 2- to 3-foot-diameter (.6- to .9-meter) circle on the sidewalk or driveway.

2. Each player places the same number of marbles in the center of the circle.

3. Using the shooter marble, a slightly larger or heavier marble called a taw, try to knock out the marbles in the middle, making sure your hand is outside the circle. Any marbles that you knock out of the circle are yours to keep.

4. Continue to shoot until you don't knock any marbles out of the circle. Leave your taw where it is (unless it rolled outside of the circle), then let the next player take a turn. If you hit another player's taw, you get all the marbles that the player has collected so far.

5. After all the marbles have been knocked out of the circle, the player with the most marbles wins.

Tip

To best shoot a marble, make a fist where your thumb knuckle is level with your index finger, and your fingers wrap over your thumb. Stick out your index finger and place your taw in the middle of your thumb knuckle. Wrap your index finger around your taw and hold it tightly. Flick your thumb to shoot the marble.

What Else to Play

Here are two other marble games you can play:

• **Bull's Eye**
Instead of shooting your marbles, drop them from eye level to knock marbles out of the circle.

• **Double Ring**
Draw a smaller circle inside a bigger one. Place the marbles in the inner circle and take turns knocking them out of both circles. If your taw ends up in the inner circle, you have to return all the marbles you've won.

Played it! ☐ Rating: ☆☆☆☆☆
Date: ___/___/_____
With: _____
Notes: _____
_____

Did You Know?
Marbles were first mass produced in the late 1800s in Ohio.

GAME NO.
47

Monkey in the Middle

This is an active and fun passing game. Keep in mind that it can easily turn into teasing if one player isn't as fast or tall as the other players, so be sure to come up with new rules for fairer play.

NUMBER OF PLAYERS:
3 or more

WHAT YOU NEED:
Ball or flying disc

WHERE TO PLAY:
Large outdoor area

ACTIVITY LEVEL:
Moderate

THE POINT OF THE GAME:
Keep the ball or flying disc away from the Monkey

How to Play

1. Pick the first player to be the Monkey. The Monkey stands inside a large circle and the rest of the players stand outside the circle.

2. The other players toss the ball or Frisbee back and forth while the Monkey tries to grab it.

3. If the Monkey intercepts the ball or Frisbee, the player who threw it becomes the new Monkey. If a player misses a catch and the Monkey grabs the ball or Frisbee, that player becomes the new Monkey.

What Else to Play

Try Monkey in the Middle in the pool! If you have a lot of people playing, choose more than one Monkey at a time.

Tip

If the Monkey is at a height disadvantage, create a rule that the other players must bounce the ball inside the circle instead of lobbing it over the Monkey's head.

Did You Know?

Monkey in the Middle is also known as Keep Away, Piggy in the Middle, Pickle in a Dish, and even Butter Blob in Denmark.

Played it! ☐ Rating: ☆☆☆☆☆
Date: ___/___/_____
With: _____
Notes: _____
_____

Mother May I?

With this game, you get to be mom, dad, or even captain for a little while.

How to Play

1. Choose a "Mother" or "Father" or "Captain" to stand with his or her back turned at one end of the play area, and the "children" at the other.

2. Children take turns asking, "Mother, may I take (certain number of steps) forward? The mother either replies "Yes, you may," or "No, you may not," and then suggests something else. So, if you ask "Mother, may I take seven giant steps forward?" The mother could say, "Yes, you may," or "No, you may not, but you can take three giant steps forward."

3. The mother could also tell her children to take steps backward if she thinks they're getting too close. The first child to reach the mother wins and becomes the new mother.

NUMBER OF PLAYERS:
3 or more

What Else to Play

In What's the Time, Mr. Wolf?, the wolf stands at one end of the play area with his or her back turned. The other children chant, "What's the time, Mr. Wolf?" If the wolf replies, "2 o'clock," the players can take two steps closer toward the wolf and so on. The first player to reach the wolf is the new wolf. If the wolf answers the chant by yelling, "Dinnertime!" the players have to run back to the start before being caught.

Tip
You can ask or be told to perform fun maneuvers, such as giant steps, baby steps, hop-like-a-frog steps, Cinderella steps (twirl in the air with each step), and more.

WHAT YOU NEED:
People

WHERE TO PLAY:
Large outdoor area

Played it! ☐ Rating: ☆☆☆☆☆

Date: ___ / ___ / _____

With: _____

Notes: _____

_____

ACTIVITY LEVEL:
Light to moderate

THE POINT OF THE GAME:
Be the first to reach "Mother"

GAME NO.

49

1, 2, 3, O'Leary

AGE LEVEL:
5 and up

NUMBER OF PLAYERS:
1 or more

WHAT YOU NEED:
Bouncing ball

WHERE TO PLAY:
Playground or other flat surface

ACTIVITY LEVEL:
Light

THE POINT OF THE GAME:
Complete the rhyme while bouncing the ball

How well can you bounce and catch a ball? Test your skills with this fun rhyming game in which you dribble a ball while passing your leg over it.

How to Play

1. The game is played to the following rhyme:

> One, two, three, O'Leary
> Four, five, six, O'Leary
> Seven, eight, nine, O'Leary
> Ten, O'Leary, catch the ball.

2. Every time you sing a number, bounce the ball with an open hand (dribbling like a basketball). When you get to "O'Leary," pass your right leg over the ball as you dribble. Catch the ball on the last line.

3. You can play by yourself or compete with others to see how many times you can get through the rhyme without messing up.

What Else to Play

There are many simple games that involve little songs or rhymes: hand-clapping games (Miss Mary Mack), jump rope games, bouncing ball games, and more.

Tip

Once you get good at this, try passing your left leg over the ball. You can also try bouncing the ball twice at each number or coming up with your own moves, such as bouncing the ball over your head and twirling around before passing your leg over the ball.

Played it! ☐ Rating: ☆☆☆☆☆
Date: ___/___/_____
With: _____
Notes: _____
_____

70

Pigs to Market

This game dates back at least 450 years. At some point long ago, sticks were used to guide actual pigs toward the finish line—an actual market!

NUMBER OF PLAYERS:
2 or more

How to Play

1. Decide on a start and finish line. Make sure each player has a long stick or broom handle and a plastic soda bottle filled with water (the "pig").
2. Racers line up at the start line with their pigs in front of them. At "Go!" the racers begin pushing their pigs along quickly with their sticks. The first player to cross the finish line with his or her pig wins.

What Else to Play

You can easily turn this into a relay race if lots of people want to play. When you tire of herding the "pigs," you can have a balancing race with each racer balancing the broomsticks on a finger as they wobble toward the finish line.

WHAT YOU NEED:
Broomsticks or long sticks, plastic 2-liter bottles filled with water

Tip

The pigs send racers zigging and zagging in each other's way trying to corral their pigs toward the finish line. This is one race where "slow and steady" might do the trick.

WHERE TO PLAY:
Large outdoor area

Played it! ☐ Rating: ☆☆☆☆☆
Date: ___/___/_____
With: _____
Notes: _____
_____

ACTIVITY LEVEL:
Moderate

THE POINT OF THE GAME:
Race with your "pig" across the finish line

51

Racing

AGE LEVEL:
4 and up

NUMBER OF PLAYERS:
2 or more

WHAT YOU NEED:
People

WHERE TO PLAY:
Large outdoor area

ACTIVITY LEVEL:
Highly Active

THE POINT OF THE GAME:
Cross the finish line first

Ready, set, go! And we're off to the races. You can race on foot, on bike or skateboard, in the pool, and even in a potato sack. You can run, crawl, slither, roll, hop, or scamper on your hands like a wheelbarrow while someone holds your feet. All you need is a start line, a finish line, and a little imagination.

How to Play

The most basic race is a foot race with a start and a finish. Someone says "go" and the first one to the finish line is the winner. For a fun variation, add actions to do at certain spots ("Twirl like a ballerina at the fire hydrant!") or make the race route a winding one with fences and trees in the way. If you have a lot of people, try a relay race with teams. Each team member takes turns running once they've been tagged by the previous runner. The first team to finish running wins. Here are some fun races to run either as individual competitions or as relays:

• Lie on your back and push yourself off the ground with your hands and feet. Crab walk your way to the finish line.
• Run a relay race where each runner has to carry a heavy bucket of water or a log. The runners have to hand off the heavy item to the next runner to cross the finish line.
• Race while jumping rope!
• Race while dribbling a basketball or soccer ball.
• Race while balancing an egg on a spoon.
• Race while riding piggyback with a teammate.
• Race while pushing a ball with your head.

Tip
Don't run races right after a big meal!

What Else to Play

On a hot, summer day, consider this fun race: Place empty buckets at the finish line and a kiddie pool filled with water at the start line. Give each runner or team a cup, and at "Go" the runners have to fill their cups with water, run to the finish line, and pour the water from their cups into the buckets. The first runner or team to fill their bucket wins. The last to finish gets buckets of water over their heads.

Played it! ☐ Rating: ☆☆☆☆☆

Date: ___/___/_____

With: _____

Notes: _____

_____

Did You Know?

Before running was a game and a form of exercise, our ancestors ran to catch food—and to avoid becoming food.

GAME NO.
52

Pilolo

AGE LEVEL:
4 and up

NUMBER OF PLAYERS:
5 or more

WHAT YOU NEED:
Coins

WHERE TO PLAY:
Large outdoor area

ACTIVITY LEVEL:
Moderate

THE POINT OF THE GAME:
Find the hidden treasures

This fun game is native to the West African nation of Ghana, and literally means "time to search for." One player hides a bunch of small sticks, stones, or coins, and the other players race to find them.

How to Play

1. Gather a bunch of coins or other small items (pebbles, game pieces, etc.)—have at least one item per player. Agree upon a start and finish line.
2. Choose a leader to hide the coins. While all the players wait at the start line with their backs turned, the leader hides the coins under branches, rocks, and leaves. The coins shouldn't be too easy (or too hard) to find.
3. When the leader says, "Pilolo!" the players turn around and race to find one of the hidden items. The goal is to find an item and race to the finish line. If another player sees that someone has found an item, that player too, may race to the finish line. The first player across becomes the new leader and may hide the next round of items.

What Else to Play

You can play Pilolo in teams. Each team hides a different object. The first team to get all of its players across the finish line wins.

Tip

If you're the first to find a coin, you may want to pretend you haven't found one and secretly work your way to the finish line. But be careful—someone else may find a coin and decide to make a run for it before you do!

Played it! ☐   Rating: ☆☆☆☆☆
Date: ___/___/_____
With: _____
Notes: _____
_____

Red Light, Green Light

GAME NO.

53

Great to play with a group of kids of different ages, this game is all about following directions and stopping and starting on a dime.

How to Play

1. Choose a player to be the light and mark the starting line. The light stands 20 to 30 feet (6.1 to 9.1 meters) away from the starting line, facing the players.
2. The light calls out "Green light!" and turns away from the players, and they start moving toward the light as quickly as possible.
3. At any point the light can yell "Red light!" and whip around to face the players. The players must freeze. Anyone the light catches moving returns to the starting line.
4. Play continues until someone tags the light without getting caught to be the next light.

What Else to Play

There's a fun South Korean version of this game called *Moogoonghwa Ggotchi Piyuht Seumneedah*. Whoever it is says the name of the game (which translates to The Rose of Sharon has Bloomed) while players attempt to tag him. If it gets tagged, the tagger must run back to the start line without getting tagged. If tagged, the player must link pinkies with it while the game continues. Another player can break the pinky link with an arm chop, but both players must run back to the start without getting caught.

Tip
In this game, being the fastest doesn't guarantee a win.

Played it! ☐ Rating: ☆☆☆☆☆

Date: ___/___/_____

With: _____

Notes: _____

_____

AGE LEVEL:
5 and up

NUMBER OF PLAYERS:
4 or more

WHAT YOU NEED:
People

WHERE TO PLAY:
Large outdoor area

ACTIVITY LEVEL:
Moderate

THE POINT OF THE GAME:
Don't get caught moving as you race toward the "light"

Outdoor Game

GAME NO.

54

Running Bases

AGE LEVEL:
7 and up

NUMBER OF PLAYERS:
4 or more

WHAT YOU NEED:
Boundary markers and a ball

WHERE TO PLAY:
Large outdoor area

ACTIVITY LEVEL:
Highly active

THE POINT OF THE GAME:
Steal bases without getting tagged

This is a great backyard game that can also be played on a sidewalk, a driveway, or even on a baseball field.

How to Play

1. Set up boundary lines about 60 feet (18 meters) apart. Decide on two catchers and have them stand at the boundary lines. All the other players are runners.

2. The catchers stand at the boundary lines and start throwing the ball to each other.

3. It's the runners' job to run from one boundary line to the other while the catchers try to hit them with the ball. If hit before crossing the line, the runner is out. The last two runners left are the new catchers.

What Else to Play

If you are playing with only a few runners, give each of them three outs before they become one of the catchers. This keeps the game flowing and everyone always playing. (No one is ever out!)

Tip

If playing on grass, runners can practice their sliding skills—a great way to avoid getting tagged. Also, to encourage runners to run, make a rule that you have to run at least every three throws.

Played it! ☐ Rating: ☆☆☆☆☆

Date: ___/___/_____

With: _____

Notes: _____

_____

The Snake Eats Its Tail

GAME NO.

55

Slither and squirm around while the head of the snake tries to catch the tail! Make sure to hang on to the person in front of you. Anyone who lets go is out!

How to Play

1. Choose one player to be the head of the snake and another to be the tail.

2. Stand in a line behind the head of the snake and hold hands (or the waist or shoulders) of the person in front of you. At "Go!" the head has to try to catch the tail while the other players squirm around to keep the two apart.

3. When the head catches the tail, that person is out and the next-to-last player becomes the new tail. Or, the head can go to the back of the line to become the new tail, and the second person in line becomes the new head.

What Else to Play

Tail Eating Snake, a game popular in Bangkok, Thailand, and other Asian cities is a popular variation. Two players stand facing each other, one acting as the father snake and one as the mother snake. Additional players, the baby snakes, stand in a line behind the mother snake while holding the waist of the person in front of them. The object is for the mother and the babies to move in unison so that the father can't catch the last baby snake at the tail.

Tip

This game can quickly turn chaotic, especially if you have lots of players. If that's the case, create two snakes. The first snake to lose its last tail wins.

AGE LEVEL:
4 and up

NUMBER OF PLAYERS:
10 or more

WHAT YOU NEED:
People

WHERE TO PLAY:
Large outdoor area

ACTIVITY LEVEL:
Highly active

THE POINT OF THE GAME:
For the head of the snake to catch its own tail

Played it! ☐ Rating: ☆☆☆☆☆
Date: ___/___/_____
With: _____
Notes: _____
_____

GAME NO.

56

Skully

This game was popular in the 1950s in the Northeastern cities of the United States. It's a little like Marbles (page 66), but with bottle caps instead of glass balls.

How to Play

1. Draw a 6-foot (1.8-meter) square box like the one on the next page. The spaces surrounding the number 13 are penalty areas called "dead zones" or "caps." Finally, draw a start line about 6 inches (15 centimeters) from the box with the number 1.

2. The object of the game is to shoot your bottle cap into each numbered square in order. Choose a player to go first, aiming to flick the bottle cap from the start line into box number 1. If the bottle cap lands completely within the box without touching any of the lines, the player gets to go again, this time aiming for box number 2. The turn is over once the bottle cap misses a box or lands on a line.

3. Players take turns making their way around the board. If a player hits another player's cap, he or she is awarded the next box and goes again. When flicking for any box, if a player ends up in one of the four dead zones, the bottle cap is stuck there until someone hits it out. The rescuer is then awarded a certain number of bonus shots.

Tip

Draw your board on the smoothest, flattest surface you can find. Sidewalks are sometimes too bumpy for a fun game. Try a smooth driveway. If you can't draw a full board, draw a smaller one with numbers going only up to 10.

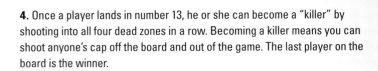

4. Once a player lands in number 13, he or she can become a "killer" by shooting into all four dead zones in a row. Becoming a killer means you can shoot anyone's cap off the board and out of the game. The last player on the board is the winner.

What Else to Play

Draw a circle and place a bunch of bottle caps in the center. Take turns flicking your bottle caps toward the caps in the circle, keeping those you successfully knock out. Whoever collects the most caps is the winner.

Played it! ☐ Rating: ☆☆☆☆☆
Date: ___/___/_____
With: _____
Notes: _____
_____

Stickball

All you need for a game of Stickball is a stick (usually a broomstick) and a Spaldeen (or other rubber bouncy ball). Follow one of the three rules based on where you're playing, and then start hitting and fielding just like baseball. This is a city game kids used to play using manhole covers for bases and buildings as foul lines. You can play it anywhere—just adjust the rules for your location!

How to Play

There are three different ways to play Stickball, and the differences are in how the ball is pitched and hit.

Fast Pitch: The batter stands in front of a wall with a strike zone marked in chalk. The pitcher throws the ball quickly and on the fly toward the batter.

Slow Pitch: The pitcher stands further away from the batter and pitches the ball with one bounce.

Fungo: The batter tosses the ball into the air himself and hits it before it hits the ground.

Whether or not you run bases or score based on how far the ball travels is up to you. Determine the rules ahead of time, and then compromise on rules as new situations come up. (What happens if the ball lands in old Mr. Mertle's yard with the big, angry dog?)

Tip

Position the field so you don't lose the ball and don't break any windows. Keep more than one ball on hand in case someone hits a home run that lands on a nearby roof.

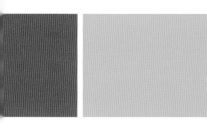

What Else to Play

If you don't have enough players for Stickball, try playing Roly Poly. The batter self-pitches, and when a fielder catches it on a fly, the fielder becomes the batter. If the fielder catches the ball on a bounce, the batter places the bat on the ground and the fielder rolls the ball toward the bat. If the ball misses the bat or hits the bat, bounces into the air, and the batter catches it, the batter gets to hit again. If the ball hits the ground before the batter can catch it, the fielder is up.

Played it! ☐ Rating: ☆☆☆☆☆

Date: ___/___/_____

With: _____

Notes: _____

_____

Did You Know?

The Native American traditional game of Stickball resembles the modern game of Lacrosse.

GAME NO.

58

Stoop Ball

AGE LEVEL:
7 and up

NUMBER OF PLAYERS:
2 or more

WHAT YOU NEED:
Spaldeen or other rubber ball

WHERE TO PLAY:
Near a stoop

ACTIVITY LEVEL:
Moderate

THE POINT OF THE GAME:
Score the most points by catching a ball thrown at a stoop

Stoop Ball is another game that became popular in the crowded cities of the 1950s. Without backyards or wide-open fields, kids invented games using what they had, which in this case was a sidewalk, a set of stairs, and a ball.

How to Play

1. Find a stoop, which is a set of stairs leading up to a building or house. (Wooden stairs don't usually work as well as cement or brick stairs.) Stand at least 5 to 7 feet from the steps. Throw the ball at one of the stairs so that the ball bounces back to you. Catch it!

2. If you catch the ball on a fly, you get 10 points. If the ball bounces on the ground once before you catch it, you get 5 points. If you miss the ball, drop it, or catch it after two or more bounces, it's the next player's turn. Keep track of your score.

3. If you hit the corner of a step, it's called a pointer. Catch a pointer on a fly and it's worth 100 points.

4. The first player to a set amount of points wins (try playing to 500 or 1,000 points).

Tip

When the ball hits a step's corner, it may come back to you as a fast line drive. It may also shoot way up into the sky. Make sure you have plenty of room to roam as you catch a pointer.

What Else to Play

There's a version of Stoop Ball that's more like a game of baseball. In this version, one player is the batter who throws the ball at the steps and the other players are the fielders. A ball caught on the fly is an out. Otherwise, hits are determined by how far the ball travels before it is fielded.

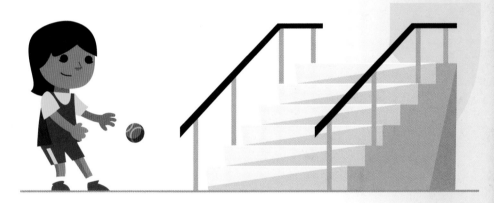

Played it! ☐ Rating: ☆☆☆☆☆

Date: ___/___/_____

With: _____

Notes: _____

_____

Did You Know?
The word "stoop" comes from the original Dutch settlers of New York.

Outdoor Game

GAME NO.

59

Tag

AGE LEVEL:
4 and up

NUMBER OF PLAYERS:
4 or more

WHAT YOU NEED:
People

WHERE TO PLAY:
Large outdoor area

ACTIVITY LEVEL:
Highly active

THE POINT OF THE GAME:
Don't get tagged

As long as the human race has been standing on two feet, we have been playing Tag. At its simplest, one player is it, and his job is to tag one of the other players and say, "Tag, you're it!" Then that player becomes the tagger. However, there are hundreds of different ways to play—you and your friends should try as many as possible. See a few favorites below.

How to Play

Cops and Robbers: Split up the players as either cops or robbers. The cops capture the robbers by tagging them and putting them in jail. If a robber can tag someone in jail without getting tagged by a cop, all the robbers are free.

Flashlight Tag: This game is played at night, and you tag someone by shining a flashlight on them.

Freeze Tag: Players who are tagged are frozen until they are unfrozen by another player.

TV Tag: This is a variation of Freeze Tag, in which a player can get unfrozen by calling out the name of a TV show. A show can only be called out once per game.

Muckle: All of the players except one are it and must tag the one player who carries a ball. When tagged, the player throws the ball in the air and whoever catches it must then run from the gang.

Zombie Tag: Start off with one or two zombies and everyone else is human. Zombies chase the humans. A human is turned into a zombie

Tip
When playing with younger kids, give them extra chances and make sure they aren't stuck as the tagger for too long.

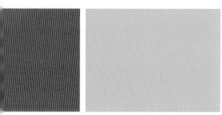

when tagged and then joins the hunt. A fun variation includes marshmallows. If a zombie is hit with a marshmallow, they are frozen for 10 seconds.

Chain Tag: Each person tagged joins hands forming a chain. The chain has to keep tagging the other players until only one person is left.

What Else to Play

Capture the Flag (page 46) is an exciting game that has elements of tag in it, as does Kick the Can (page 62).

Played it! ☐ Rating: ☆☆☆☆☆

Date: ___/___/_____

With: _____

Notes: _____

_____

Did You Know?

Gorillas play tag! One ape will hit another one and run away. The other will chase the first and try to hit back. Then they reverse rolls.

GAME NO.

60

SPUD

NUMBER OF PLAYERS:
4 or more

WHAT YOU NEED:
Dodgeball or other large, soft ball

WHERE TO PLAY:
Large outdoor area

ACTIVITY LEVEL:
Highly Active

THE POINT OF THE GAME:
Don't spell "SPUD"

Why is this game called "SPUD?" No one knows! You certainly wouldn't want to play with a potato instead of a soft ball. That would hurt.

How to Play

1. Pick the first player to be it. It stands in the middle of the playing area with the ball. All of the other players gather around.

2. It tosses the ball high into the air, calling another player's name. The named player must catch the ball while the others run away.

3. The named player catches the ball and yells "SPUD!" At that moment, the other players must freeze in place.

4. The player with the ball can take up to three giant steps to get closer to any one of the frozen players, then gets to throw the ball at the chosen person's feet. The frozen player cannot move.

5. If the ball hits the frozen player, he gets an "S" and becomes it. If the ball misses the frozen player, it gets an "S" and is it for another round.

6. The last player to spell out "SPUD" wins.

Tip
Make sure players are throwing the ball high into the air to give players enough time to run away.

What Else to Play

In Argentina, they play a game called *Alto Ahi!*, which means "Stop There!" In this version of SPUD, it calls out the name of one player when catching the ball. Only that person must freeze. When hit three times, a player is required to do something funny like making animal sounds or touching their nose with their tongue!

Played it! ☐ Rating: ☆☆☆☆☆

Date: ___ / ___ / _____

With: _____

Notes: _____

_____

Around the World

Whether on a basketball court or in your driveway, this game improves shooting from all angles. Win the game by making every shot before the other players.

How to Play

1. Mark ten spots on the basketball court with chalk and choose the first shooter.

2. Shoot from the first spot. If you make it, move to the next spot and shoot again.

3. If you miss a shot, you can either attempt a second shot, or end your turn. If you make the second shot, move onto the next spot. If you miss the second shot, you have to start over from the first shooting spot on your next turn. However, if you skip your second shot, you can start from the spot you left off on your next turn.

What Else to Play

If you're all a bunch of sharpshooters, go around the world and back again. The first player to hit all shots from one to ten and back again wins. This game (as well as H-O-R-S-E on page 88) is also fun to play with mini hoops that you can set up indoors.

Tip
Know your limitations! It's fun to gamble on making a second shot, but if it's a shot you're not that good at, you may want to stay where you are and wait until your turn comes around again.

Played it! ☐ Rating: ☆☆☆☆☆
Date: ___/___/_____
With: _____
Notes: _____
_____

AGE LEVEL:
7 and up

NUMBER OF PLAYERS:
2 or more

WHAT YOU NEED:
Basketball, hoop, chalk

WHERE TO PLAY:
Basketball court

ACTIVITY LEVEL:
Moderate

THE POINT OF THE GAME:
Make it around the world by making your shots

GAME NO.
62

H-O-R-S-E

AGE LEVEL:
7 and up

NUMBER OF PLAYERS:
2 or more

WHAT YOU NEED:
Basketball

WHERE TO PLAY:
Basketball court

ACTIVITY LEVEL:
Light to moderate

THE POINT OF THE GAME:
Make more matching shots than your opponent

If you don't have enough players for a pick-up game of basketball, or you just want to practice shooting, try a game of Horse. There are no animals involved, but this game does feel like you're just horsing around. And remember that as with all games, you whinny some and you lose some.

How to Play

1. Decide who will go first. This player creates a set-up shot from anywhere on the court. The shot could also include extra rules. For instance, you can say, "this shot is with your eyes closed" or "you have to shoot this with your non-dominant hand."

2. If the shot doesn't go in, the next player gets to choose a set-up shot to attempt.

3. If the shot goes in, all of the other players must copy the shot exactly.

4. Each player who misses the shot gets an "H." Once you have spelled out "horse" due to missed shots, you're out of the game. Keep playing until there is only one player left.

What Else to Play

If you don't have a lot of time to play H-O-R-S-E, you can play P-I-G or G-O-A-T instead. And see page 87 for another great basketball shooting game.

Tip

If you're not a great shooter, keep setting up the other players with easy shots. The game will take longer, but as long as you're in control, you can't lose!

Played it! ☐ Rating: ☆☆☆☆☆
Date: ___/___/_____
With: _____
Notes: _____
_____

Shark and Minnows

Outdoor Game

GAME NO.

63

Shark and Minnows is a fun variation of tag that you play in the pool! Avoid the shark in the center of the pool by swimming as fast as you can.

AGE LEVEL:
7 and up

How to Play

1. Pick a shark. Everyone else is a minnow. The minnows line up on one side of the pool while the shark swims around the middle.

2. When the shark yells, "Swim!" all of the minnows jump into the water and swim as fast as they can to the other side of the pool. The shark tags as many minnows as possible.

3. When minnows gets caught, they stay in the middle of the pool with the shark and help tag more minnows.

4. The game continues until all the minnows are caught.

NUMBER OF PLAYERS:
5 or more

WHAT YOU NEED:
People

What Else to Play

As a fun variation, tagged minnows can become seaweed instead of sharks. Players who become seaweed cannot swim away, but can tag minnows to also become seaweed. If seaweed tag the shark, they become a minnow again and can swim to safety. You can also try playing on land! Choose starting and finishing lines, with the shark in the middle.

Tip
Instead of having the other minnows become sharks, they can be out.

WHERE TO PLAY:
A pool

Played it! ☐ Rating: ☆☆☆☆☆

Date: ___/___/_____

With: _____

Notes: _____

_____

ACTIVITY LEVEL:
Highly active

THE POINT OF THE GAME:
Don't get tagged by the shark

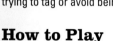

Outdoor Game

GAME NO.

64

Marco Polo

AGE LEVEL:
6 and up

NUMBER OF PLAYERS:
4 or more

WHAT YOU NEED:
People

WHERE TO PLAY:
A pool

ACTIVITY LEVEL:
Moderate

THE POINT OF THE GAME:
Avoid getting tagged

This is one of the most popular pool games ever! All you need are a bunch of friends and a pool. The rules are simple and you'll get a lot of exercise trying to tag or avoid being tagged.

How to Play

1. Pick a player to be the caller. The caller closes his or her eyes (and keeps them closed) and the other players swim away.

2. The caller calls out "Marco!" and all of the other players have to respond by calling out "Polo!" Without peeking, the caller must follow the sounds of the other players' voices and try to tag someone. The players can swim around, but they have to yell "Polo" each time the caller yells "Marco."

3. The first player to be tagged is the new caller.

Tip

If you're playing in a large pool or have only a few people playing, put a time limit on being a caller. Not being able to tag anyone for too long can lead to frustration.

What Else to Play

Blind Tag is a lot like Marco Polo, except there's no call and response. This is perfect for playing in smaller pools or for younger players. The players can either remain frozen in place or swim around. No pool? No problem. Play a game of Blind Man's Bluff, which is Marco Polo on land where the person who's it wears a blindfold. Just make sure to play where the blindfolded player `can't get hurt.

Played it! ☐ Rating: ☆☆☆☆☆

Date: ___/___/_____

With: _____

Notes: _____

_____

90

Charades

GAME NO.

65

Silence is golden in this game that first gained popularity way back in the 18th century in France. Players divide into two teams and act out words or phrases without talking.

How to Play

1. Divide your group into two teams (they don't have to be even).
2. Give everyone slips of paper and pens, and ask them to write down a word or phrase to act out. You can choose animals, books, TV shows, movie or song titles, or even well-known phrases.
3. Fold up the slips and put them in a bowl or box.
4. The first team up elects a player to act first, who chooses a slip from the bowl.
5. Set the timer for 90 seconds, then go! Without speaking, the player has to act out the phrase. His or her team can shout out their answers. The round is up when the team guesses correctly, or time runs out.

What Else to Play

Heads Up! is a charades game you can play on a smartphone. When it's your turn, your team can see the word or phrase and has to act it out for you. Just hold the phone up to your forehead to show your team the clue.

Did You Know?

You can find tons of tips on how to play online, such as common ways to let your team know the category (for a book, open your palms and pretend to turn pages).

AGE LEVEL:
3 and up

NUMBER OF PLAYERS:
4 or more

WHAT YOU NEED:
Stopwatch, paper slips, pens or pencils, bowl

WHERE TO PLAY:
Anywhere

ACTIVITY LEVEL:
Light

THE POINT OF THE GAME:
Act out a word or phrase so your team can guess it correctly within the time limit

Played it! ☐ Rating: ☆☆☆☆☆
Date: ___/___/_____
With: _____
Notes: _____
_____

GAME NO.
66

Cranium

AGE LEVEL:
13 and up

NUMBER OF PLAYERS:
4 to 16

WHAT YOU NEED:
Cranium game

WHERE TO PLAY:
Indoors

ACTIVITY LEVEL:
Light

THE POINT OF THE GAME:
Move your game piece to the center of the board by successfully completing challenges

Your cranium is your skull; the board game Cranium makes you use every piece of what's inside your skull! It calls on players to use skills needed to play charades, Pictionary, Trivial Pursuit, word games, Claymania, Celebrities, and more. This game is perfect for family gatherings and parties—the more players, the more hilarious the experience.

How to Play

You need at least two teams of two players to play, but you can create up to four teams. Teams have to successfully complete activities in order to move their pieces toward the center of the game board. The activities come from four sets of themed cards. With the Creative Cat cards, players try to make their team guess a word by drawing it, sculpting it in clay, or drawing it with their eyes closed. With the Data Head cards, teams must answer a trivia question. With the Word Worm cards, players have to unscramble words, spell them backwards, guess definitions, and more. With the Star Performer cards, players must whistle a song, impersonate a celebrity, or act out a clue. The first team to successfully complete enough activities to get to the center of the game board wins.

What Else to Play

If you liked the Data Head cards, play Trivial Pursuit. Star Power? Try Time's Up! Word Worm? Try Balderdash. Creative Cat? Definitely play some Pictionary.

Tip
Know your strengths and try to avoid categories you know your team will struggle with.

Played it! ☐ Rating: ☆☆☆☆☆

Date: ___/___/_____

With: _____

Notes: _____

_____

Did You Know?

Cranium Conga was created so that younger family members (8 and up) could join in the fun.

GAME NO.

67

Celebrity

AGE LEVEL:
8 and up

This three-round party game relies on many skills including acting, memorization, and expert clue giving. The more people you have for this game, the better.

NUMBER OF PLAYERS:
4 to 16

WHAT YOU NEED:
Paper, pencils, timer, hat or box

How to Play

1. Before play begins, have each player write the names of five celebrities on five pieces of paper. A celebrity can be a famous person, animal, or even a fictional character. All the slips of paper are put in a hat or box.

2. One team is chosen to go first, and one player on that team is chosen to give clues to the rest of the team. The clue giver has one minute to get teammates to guess as many names in the hat or box as possible. In round one, the clue giver can give almost any sort of hint but cannot pass on a celebrity. Once time is up, the next team goes, using the celebrities in the hat the first team didn't get to. Play continues until the teams guess all the celebrities. Teams get one point for each celebrity.

3. In round two, the celebrities are put back in the hat. This time, the clue givers only use one word for each hint, and teammates can only give one answer. The clue giver can pass on celebrities that teammates have trouble with.

4. In round three, with the celebrities back in the hat, the clue givers play charades to guess all the celebrities. The clue giver can pass and teams give one answer per celebrity.

5. The team with the most points after three rounds is the winner.

WHERE TO PLAY:
Anywhere

Tip

The best way to help your team is to give good clues in round one. This way, the team will have an easier time in the next rounds remembering the celebrities in the hat.

ACTIVITY LEVEL:
Light

THE POINT OF THE GAME:
Guess as many celebrity names as possible before time runs out

What Else to Play

If you don't have time to play all three rounds, you can decide to play only round one or charades. Round two is difficult to play on its own. Also, there are a few board game versions of Celebrity, including Time's Up!, Monikers, and Celebrity Name Game.

Played it! ☐ Rating: ☆☆☆☆☆

Date: ___/___/_____

With: _____

Notes: _____

_____

Tip

During round one, clue givers must avoid saying any part of the celebrity's name. Doing so ends the round for that team. (If you want to be nice about it, it could be a pass instead.)

GAME NO.

68

Crazy Eights

THE POINT
OF THE GAME:
Get rid of all the cards
in your hand

This game is also called Switch, Eights, or Swedish Rummy. The eights are "crazy" because they are wild.

How to Play

1. Deal seven cards to each player facedown, and place the rest of the deck facedown in the middle of the table. This is the stockpile.

2. Turn the top card of the stockpile faceup. (This card cannot be an eight! If you do draw an eight, put it back in the deck and draw again.)

3. The player to the left of the dealer goes first. On your turn, you must play a card that is the same suit or rank as the faceup card. If you don't have either, you can play a wild eight card to choose the next suit. If you don't have an eight, you must draw from the stockpile until you get a card you can play.

4. The round ends when a player has no more cards or when no one can make any more plays, in which case the player holding cards with the lowest total value wins the hand. The round winner is awarded points based on the cards left in the other players' hands: 50 points for any eights, 10 points for any face cards or aces, and the face value for all other cards.

5. Keep playing hands until someone gets 250 or 500 points, depending on how long you want to play.

Tip
Save your eights for as long as possible!

What Else to Play

Make things a little more fun by adding some of your own rules! For example, make a certain number reverse play, skip the next player, or require players to touch their nose. You can also try your hand at the similar card game Uno (page 123).

Played it! ☐ Rating: ☆☆☆☆☆

Date: ___/___/_____

With: _____

Notes: _____

_____

Did You Know?

Crazy Eights first appeared in the 1930s and was originally just called Eights.

GAME NO.

69

Gin Rummy

AGE LEVEL:
5 and up

This matching card game is similar to many games played around the world, including Mahjong, Canasta, and the popular Phase 10. The point is pretty simple—create the most combinations of cards to win!

NUMBER OF PLAYERS:
2 to 4

WHAT YOU NEED:
Standard deck of cards

How to Play

1. If playing with 2 people, deal ten cards to each player. If playing with 3 or more, deal seven cards.
2. The top card from the stockpile is turned over to create a discard pile.
3. Players organize their cards into possible combinations. A combination can either be three or more cards of the same suit in consecutive order (6, 7, and 8 of spades) or three or more cards of the same rank (three Jacks).
4. The player to the left of the dealer goes first. On your turn, pick up the top card from the discard pile or from the stockpile, and discard a card from your hand. Try to use the new card in a combination.
5. The player who can use all of his or her cards except for one in a combination wins. The leftover card is thrown onto the discard pile and the player says, "Gin!" Each winning hand is worth 25 points. Play until someone reaches 100 or 150 points.

Tip
If you believe someone else is trying to create the same combination as you, try not to discard cards that will get them closer to a win.

WHERE TO PLAY:
Flat surface

What Else to Play

Rummy 500 is played similarly. Lay your combinations as you create them, and other players can add cards to your combinations.

ACTIVITY LEVEL:
Minimal

THE POINT OF THE GAME:
Create card combinations to get rid of your cards

Played it! ☐ Rating: ☆☆☆☆☆
Date: ___/___/_____
With: _____
Notes: _____
_____

War

Go head-to-head to collect all the cards! This is a simple game you will get the hang of very quickly.

AGE LEVEL:
4 and up

How to Play

1. Give each player half the deck. No peeking!

2. Both players turn over their top cards at the same time and place them side by side, faceup. The one who plays the higher-ranking card gets to keep both cards. Aces are the high card in this game.

3. When both players turn over cards of the same rank (two Jacks, for instance), the players go to war. Each player places the top three cards from their piles facedown, then places a fourth card faceup on the table. The person with the higher card wins all the cards played.

4. The player who captures all 52 cards wins.

NUMBER OF PLAYERS:
2

WHAT YOU NEED:
Standard deck of cards

What Else to Play

Try this fun variation! When War is declared, instead of the higher card winning, one or both players must flip over cards that add up to 15 (face cards equal 10 points and Aces 1). Any player who goes over 15 points loses the hand. If both players go over 15, start a new war.

Did You Know?

War is similar to the British card game Beggar-my-neighbour, which appears in Charles Dickens's 1861 novel *Great Expectations*.

WHERE TO PLAY:
Flat surface

ACTIVITY LEVEL:
Minimal

Played it! ☐ Rating: ☆☆☆☆☆
Date: ___/___/_____
With: _____
Notes: _____
_____

THE POINT OF THE GAME:
Capture all your opponent's cards

Solitaire

WHERE TO
PLAY:
Flat surface

ACTIVITY
LEVEL:
Minimal

THE POINT
OF THE GAME:
Sort the cards into
four piles in ascending
order by suit

There are hundreds of ways to play cards by yourself. These games, known as Solitaire, have been around forever, but the most popular solitaire game is called Klondike, which rose to fame in the late 1800s during the gold rush. The goal is to sort the deck by suit from Ace (low card) up to King.

How to Play

1. To set up, create seven stacks from left to right, with each stack containing one more card than the last. The first stack has one upturned card. The second has one downturned and one upturned. The third has two downturned and one upturned. And so on. Place the remaining deck above the stacks on the left side—you'll use this stockpile when you run out of moves during play.

2. Each suit is placed above the piles created in step one. These four spots are called foundations.

3. Sort the faceup cards in the seven stacks by alternating red and black cards in sequence. For example, a black nine can be transferred on top of a red ten. Flip over any facedown cards at the top of the stacks. If you uncover an ace, place it in one of the four foundation piles.

4. If you have an empty pile, you can transfer a King (or a pile of cards that start with a King) to that space.

5. Once you've moved all that you can on the stacks, turn three cards over at once from the stockpile. Sort the top card on your stacks, if you can. Then sort the second card, then the third. If you can't use the cards, return them to the bottom of the stock pile.

6. Keep playing until you build the four suits from Ace to King or you can no longer make any moves.

What Else to Play

Other popular Solitaire games include Anno Domini, Fascination, Marguerite, the Royal Windows, Perseverance, the Privileged Four, the Wheel, and so many more. Look them up!

Played it! ☐ Rating: ☆☆☆☆☆

Date: ___/___/_____

With: _____

Notes: _____

_____

Did You Know?
In Britain, this game is known as Patience.

GAME NO.
72

Old Maid

Old Maid is fun for the entire family! While there are specialized decks you can buy, a standard deck of cards works perfectly.

How to Play

1. Begin by removing three of the Queens from the deck. The remaining Queen is the Old Maid. (You can play Old Miser by removing three Kings instead.)

2. Deal the whole deck facedown to players. Look at your cards, and pull out any pairs, placing them facedown.

3. Players take turns fanning out and offering their cards to the player to their left, who must choose one of the cards. If the card matches one of the cards in that player's hand, he or she puts the pair facedown in a pile.

4. Play continues until all of the cards have been paired, except for the Queen—the player left holding the Old Maid loses.

What Else to Play

To add an element of surprise to the game, instead of removing the queens, remove a random card from the deck without anyone seeing it. Now no one knows which card is the Old Maid. For instance, if you remove the 2 of hearts, the other red 2—the 2 of diamonds—becomes the Old Maid card. In the Philippines, this variant is called *Ungguy-ungguyan*.

Tip
This game is all luck, so it's great to play with younger kids.

Played it! ☐ Rating: ☆☆☆☆☆
Date: ___/___/_____
With: _____
Notes: _____
_____

Slapjack

All you need for Slapjack are lightning-fast reflexes! Be the first to recognize and slap a Jack when you see one.

How to Play
1. Deal the full deck to the players facedown. No peeking!
2. The player to the left of the dealer goes first. On your turn, play the top card from your pile. The next player does the same. Once a player plays a Jack, all the players try to slap the card. Gentle slaps only, please!
3. The first one to slap the Jack takes the whole pile of faceup cards and mixes them in their deck.
4. The player to the left of the winner starts again.

What Else to Play
For an older crowd, try a game of Egyptian Ratscrew. Each player takes turns playing a card. Once someone plays a face card, the next player has a fixed number of chances to turn up another face card (Ace, four chances; King, three chances; Queen, two chances; Jack, one chance.) If the player fails to turn up a face card, the previous player keeps the cards. If the player succeeds, the next player has the same number of chances to turn up a face card, and so on.

Tip
If you run out of cards, you can still wait to slap the next Jack in order to get some cards back. However, if you miss it, then you're out.

AGE LEVEL:
5 and up

NUMBER OF PLAYERS:
2 to 5

WHAT YOU NEED:
Standard deck of cards

WHERE TO PLAY:
Flat surface

ACTIVITY LEVEL:
Minimal

THE POINT OF THE GAME:
Win all the cards

Played it! ☐ Rating: ☆☆☆☆☆
Date: ___/___/_____
With: _____
Notes: _____
_____

GAME NO.

74

Spit

AGE LEVEL:
6 and up

NUMBER OF PLAYERS:
2

WHAT YOU NEED:
Standard deck of cards

WHERE TO PLAY:
Flat surface

ACTIVITY LEVEL:
Light

THE POINT OF THE GAME:
Get rid of all your cards

This lightning-fast game is a mad free-for-all attempt to get rid of your cards before your opponent does.

How to Play

1. Each player gets 26 cards. Set up 15 of your 26 cards in five stacks, where the first stack has 1 card, the second 2, and so on. The remaining 11 cards are kept facedown to the right of the stacks. This is your deck.

2. When both players are ready, yell "Spit!" and place the top cards from your decks faceup in the middle of the table next to each other. This forms two discard piles.

3. Using only one hand, place as many cards as you can on top of either discard pile from your five stacks as fast as you can. In order to place a card on the discard pile, it must be either one higher or one lower than the top card on the pile. For example, you can place either a 6 or an 8 on top of a 7 card. Aces are high and low so you could place either a King or a 2 on an Ace.

4. Once you've played the top card from one of your stacks, flip the new top card so it's turned faceup. You can combine cards in your stacks if they are the same rank. If one of your stacks is empty, you can also move one of the top cards from a stack onto the empty space and then flip the top card of that stack up. (This allows you to open more of your cards to play.)

5. When both players can't make any more moves, one player yells, "Spit!" and you both move one card from the top of your decks onto the discard piles and resume play.

Tip

Not only do you have to keep an eye on what you're doing, you also have to make sure the other player isn't making any illegal moves!

6. The round finishes when one player plays all the cards in his or her stacks. The player who finishes first takes the smaller (but no counting cards!) discard pile and the other player gets the other one.

7. Add the cards to your decks without shuffling and play again. When one player has a few cards left, continue play with only one discard pile. The first player to get rid of all cards wins.

What Else to Play

If you love fast-paced card games, check out Slapjack (page 103), Spoons (page 106), and Snap (page 108).

Played it! ☐ Rating: ☆☆☆☆☆

Date: ___/___/_____

With: _____

Notes: _____

_____

Did You Know?
Spit is also known as Speed and Slam.

GAME NO.

75

Spoons

Spoons is one intense, pressure-filled game where the more people you have, the more crazy fun you will have. The goal is to achieve a four of a kind—four Kings, four 2s, etc.—and grab a spoon before anyone else does.

NUMBER OF PLAYERS:
4 to 12

WHAT YOU NEED:
Deck of cards, Spoons

How to Play

1. Place enough spoons for each player, minus one, in the center of the table. Deal each player four cards. Place the rest of the deck near the dealer.

2. The dealer takes a card from the deck and either discards this card or another card from his or her hand, placing it facedown next to the player to the left.

3. The second player then picks up that card and either discards it or another card from his or her hand and places it facedown next to the player to the left. And so on. Meanwhile the dealer keeps picking up cards from the deck and discarding cards. The last player to receive a card places one card in a trash pile. This creates a constant stream of cards coming and going from your hand.

4. Once a player has four of a kind, he or she picks up a spoon. That gives the rest of the players the freedom to grab a spoon—even if they don't have a four of a kind. Any player left without a spoon at the end of a round is out. You can also play so that the person without a spoon gets an S, and after a few rounds, the player who spells out SPOON is out.

WHERE TO PLAY:
Flat surface

Tip

The first player who gets four of a kind can either be sneaky or obvious about taking a spoon. He or she can pretend to keep playing the game by taking cards and discarding them, or cause a spoon-grabbing panic!

ACTIVITY LEVEL:
Light

THE POINT OF THE GAME:
Don't be left without a spoon

What Else to Play

Try Extreme Spoons: place the spoons someplace nearby but inconvenient—leading to a mad race to the spoons. Or you can play Pig, where instead of grabbing a spoon, the first person to get four of a kind quietly puts a finger on the tip of his or her nose.

Played it! ☐ Rating: ☆☆☆☆☆

Date: ___/___/_____

With: _____

Notes: _____

_____

Did You Know?
Spoons are really old! Their use goes back to ancient Egyptian times.

GAME NO.
76

Snap

AGE LEVEL:
6 and up

NUMBER OF PLAYERS:
2 to 4

WHAT YOU NEED:
Standard deck of cards

WHERE TO PLAY:
Flat surface

ACTIVITY LEVEL:
Minimal

THE POINT OF THE GAME:
Win all the cards and make a lot of noise

In this fast-paced and noisy game, try to win all the cards!

How to Play

1. Deal out all the cards facedown. No peeking!

2. Players take turns flipping over the card at the top of their pile and placing it faceup in a new pile.

3. When someone turns over a card that matches a card already faceup on another player's pile, the players race to yell "Snap!" The first to do so wins both piles and adds the cards to the bottom of their facedown pile.

4. If two players yell "Snap!" at the same time, the two piles are combined and placed in the center of the table with one of the two matching cards on top. This is called the Snap Pot. When someone turns a card that matches the card on top of the Snap Pot, the first person to yell "Snap Pot!" wins that pile.

5. The player who wins all the cards wins the game.

What Else to Play

Instead of yelling "Snap," have each player come up with an animal noise to make. Check out Spit (page 104) and Slapjack (page 103), two other fast-paced games!

Tip

Be careful! If you call "Snap!" at the wrong time, you must give a card to each player as punishment.

Played it! ☐ Rating: ☆☆☆☆☆
Date: ___/___/_____
With: _____
Notes: _____
_____

Go Fish

Go Fish is probably one of the first card games you learned to play. The official rules, however, might be a little different from what you may remember! Collect all four cards of the same rank before anyone else to win.

How to Play

1. If playing with up to three players, each player gets seven cards. If playing with four or more, each gets five cards. Place the remaining cards spread out facedown on the table.

2. The player to the left of the dealer starts the game. Ask any player for any cards you need to make a group of four. If the other player has the cards, he or she must hand them over, and you can ask another player for cards.

3. If the other player doesn't have the cards you ask for, he or she says, "Go Fish," and you can take a card from the fishing pond, ending your turn. The player who said "Go Fish" is next to ask for cards.

4. Play continues until all the cards are matched up. The player with the most matching cards at the end of the game wins.

What Else to Play

If you are playing with really young children, collect pairs instead of four of a kind. For a more advanced card collecting game, try Gin Rummy (page 98).

Tip

Pay attention to what the other players are collecting!

Played it! ☐ Rating: ☆☆☆☆☆
Date: ___/___/_____
With: _____
Notes: _____
_____

THE POINT OF THE GAME:
Collect the most matching cards

GAME NO.

78

Go

Go is an ancient game that is considered more complex than chess. Professional games can take up to 16 hours to complete, but you can play with a friend in an hour or less.

How to Play

A Go board is a grid of 19 horizontal and vertical lines. There are 181 black pieces and 180 white pieces. Pieces are played where the grid lines intersect. Black always goes first, and the players take turns placing their pieces. Once you place a piece, you can't move it. The goal is to capture more territory than the other player, and this is done by creating and defending your territory, attacking your opponent's territory, and also by surrounding and capturing your opponent's pieces. The rules can be a bit tricky, but once you get the hang of it, you'll find yourself in a life-and-death battle of strategy that has more moves and surprises than you can imagine.

NUMBER OF PLAYERS:
2 to 10

WHAT YOU NEED:
Go board and game pieces

What Else to Play

Go-Muku uses a Go board and pieces, but the rules are quite simple. Players compete to be the first to place five of one's own pieces in a row along a horizontal, vertical, or diagonal line.

WHERE TO PLAY:
Flat surface

Tip

Let inexperienced players be black, and let them put down more than one piece during their first turn. If both players are inexperienced, start on a 9" x 9" board first.

ACTIVITY LEVEL:
Minimal

THE POINT OF THE GAME:
Surround your opponent's pieces with your own

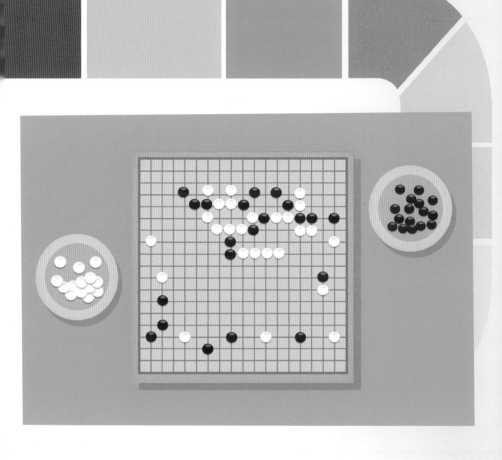

Did You Know?

In 2015, a master Go player was finally beaten by a computer—Google's AlphaGo artificial intelligence program. Until then, the game was considered too complicated for a computer to win.

GAME NO.

79

Apples to Apples

AGE LEVEL:
12 and up

NUMBER OF PLAYERS:
4 to 10

WHAT YOU NEED:
Apples to Apples game

WHERE TO PLAY:
Flat surface

ACTIVITY LEVEL:
Minimal

THE POINT OF THE GAME:
Win the most rounds by playing the best red cards to match the green cards

This is a hilarious game of surprising and outrageous comparisons where there are no right or wrong answers—just a bunch of very opinionated judges! Most players care more about making people laugh than actually winning, making this a great game. It's also easy to learn (it's as easy as comparing apples to apples!) and doesn't have a lot of rules. Whether you have thirty minutes to spare or three hours, Apples to Apples is one of those games you simply have to have in your game closet.

How to Play

Apples to Apples consists of a pack of green adjective (descriptions) cards and a pack of red noun (people, places, things, and events) cards. A judge picks a green card from the top of the deck and places it on the table. The players—except for the player judging the round—all play one of the seven red cards in their hands that best fits the green card. The judge decides who wins that round with the best noun. For example, the judge places a green card "Depressing" on the table. The players choose the following nouns: "Noisy Neighbors," "My Bathroom," "Girl Scouts," "Pigeons," and "the Dallas Cowboys." The judge gets to pick the winner, no matter what. Which would you choose?

Tip

While the judge is deciding, you're allowed to lobby for your red card. You can argue, cajole, and ridicule other people's answers. And remember, it's not always about what's the best answer, but what's the best answer for that particular judge!

What Else to Play

The T-Shirt Game is a bit like Apples to Apples, but instead of nouns and adjectives, players submit ridiculous slogans or captions based on outrageous T-shirt designs.

Played it! ☐ Rating: ☆☆☆☆☆

Date: ___ / ___ / _____

With: _____

Notes: _____

_____

Did You Know?

There are several versions of Apples to Apples, including Junior and Kids for younger players, Sour Apples to Apples (where the worst answer incurs a penalty), and even a Bible edition.

GAME NO.

80

Backgammon

AGE LEVEL:
6 and up

Of all the old games in this book, Backgammon is one of the oldest. It can be dated back to 3000 BC!

How to Play

1. Place your 15 pieces on the 24 triangles, or points, on the board.

2. You and your opponent alternate moving your pieces around the board according to the rolls of the dice. If you roll a 5 and a 3, you must move one piece five points and another piece three points. The same piece can be moved twice, as long as the two moves can be made separately.

3. You may land on any point that is unoccupied by the opponent's pieces or on a point where you have your own pieces. You can also land on a point where there is only one of the opponent's pieces. This is called "hitting a blot." When you hit a blot, the opponent's blot piece is placed in the middle of the board on the bar that divides the two sides of the playing surface. The opponent cannot move the rest of their pieces until they are able to move the piece back on the board.

4. Once you have all of your pieces on your home board, you can start to remove them, or bear them off, with rolls of the dice. The first player to bear off all their pieces wins.

NUMBER OF PLAYERS:
2

WHAT YOU NEED:
Backgammon game

WHERE TO PLAY:
Flat surface

Tip

Even though this is a dice game, there is a lot of strategy involved. You can block your opponent from moving onto points by having more than one piece on a point, you can try to make sure you have more than one piece on any one point to avoid getting blotted, and more.

ACTIVITY LEVEL:
Minimal

THE POINT OF THE GAME:
Be the first to remove all your pieces from the board

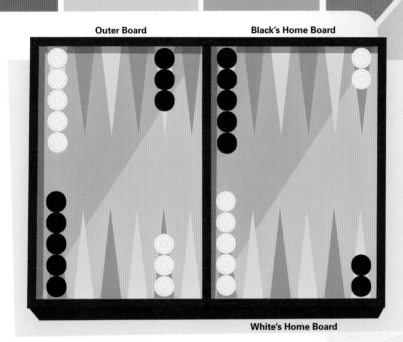

Outer Board   Black's Home Board

White's Home Board

What Else to Play

There are many different variations of Backgammon. Younger children can play Blast Off, which is regular Backgammon without hitting blots. Or, try Hyper Backgammon, which is played with just three pieces per player, set up on your opponent's one-point, two-point, and three-point.

Played it! ☐ Rating: ☆☆☆☆☆

Date: ___/___/_____

With: _____

Notes: _____

_____

Did You Know?

During the 1500s, Backgammon was banned in Europe by the Catholic church, so people started creating foldable boards to hide the game. Today, the game is still played with hinged boards.

GAME NO.

81

Checkers

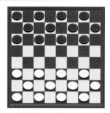

When you play Checkers, you're playing a game that dates back 5,000 years. Sometimes, that's how long it feels like you're waiting for your opponent's next move!

NUMBER OF PLAYERS:
2

How to Play

1. Each player starts with 12 pieces (usually red or black) placed on a board with 32 dark squares and 32 light squares. The pieces are positioned as shown.

2. The object is to capture your opponent's pieces by moving diagonally along the dark squares and jumping over your opponent's pieces when possible. Black goes first, and players alternate turns.

3. You can only move forward one square at a time, unless you are jumping over one of your opponent's pieces. When a piece is captured, it is removed from the board.

WHAT YOU NEED:
Checker board and pieces

4. If one of your pieces reaches the opposite side of the board, it becomes a king, and your opponent places one of your captured pieces on top of it. A King can move backward as well as forward.

5. If a player is able to make a capture, the jump must be made. Play continues until all of one player's pieces have been captured.

WHERE TO PLAY:
Flat surface

What Else to Play

Checkers is also known as Draughts. International Draughts is played on a 10 x 10 board with 20 pieces each.

ACTIVITY LEVEL:
Minimal

Tip

When first learning to play, keep your pieces toward the middle of the board in the form of a pyramid. Pieces on the sides can only move in one direction, which limits move options.

THE POINT OF THE GAME:
Capture your opponent's pieces

Played it! ☐ Rating: ☆☆☆☆☆
Date: ___/___/_____
With: _____
Notes: _____
_____

Chess

Chess is like a medieval fantasy come to life. Two kingdoms battle it out using strategy, cunning, and brute strength until one of the Kings is captured. It may take a little while getting used to how the pieces move, but once you get the hang of it, you'll get better each time you play.

AGE LEVEL:
8 and up

How to Play

Chess is played on a 64-square board. Each player has 16 pieces: 1 King, 1 Queen, 2 Bishops, 2 Knights, 2 Rooks or Castles, and 8 Pawns. Each piece has specific ways to move on the board. Using the knowledge of how your pieces move, plan your attack against your opponent. Players take turns moving their pieces to try to capture their opponent's pieces. The goal is to checkmate the King, which means the King can no longer move without being captured. Here's how the pieces move:

King: Moves one square at a time in any direction.

Queen: The most powerful piece, the queen moves any number of squares in any direction.

Bishop: Moves any number of squares diagonally.

Knight: Moves in an L-shape and can jump over another piece.

Rook: Moves in a straight line.

Pawn: Moves forward one square at a time (for the first move of the game, a pawn may move two squares.)

NUMBER OF PLAYERS:
2

WHAT YOU NEED:
Chess board and pieces

What Else to Play

Check out these other good strategy games to play next: Settlers of Catan (page 130), Pandemic (page 123), and Mu Torere (page 15).

WHERE TO PLAY:
Flat surface

Played it! ☐   Rating: ☆☆☆☆☆

Date: ___/___/_____

With: _____

Notes: _____

_____

ACTIVITY LEVEL:
Minimal

THE POINT OF THE GAME:
Capture your opponent's king

GAME NO.
83

Clue

NUMBER
OF PLAYERS:
3 to 6

WHAT YOU
NEED:
Clue game board

WHERE TO
PLAY:
Flat surface

ACTIVITY
LEVEL:
Minimal

THE POINT
OF THE GAME:
Solve the mystery of
who killed Mr. Boddy

Was it Colonel Mustard in the study with the candlestick? Or Miss Scarlet in the library with the revolver? If you're a crime-solving wiz, or even if you just love a good mystery, you'll love playing Clue. Each player gets to be a suspect, exploring Tudor Mansion to find out who killed the doomed Mr. Boddy. Gather your evidence and get ready to solve a murder!

How to Play

1. Each player chooses a suspect to represent, and is given some clues from the card deck. The key to the mystery is hidden in the Confidential Case File.

2. Players move around the board, through each room in the mansion. On each turn, you can suggest who might have committed the murder.

3. Take notes on your Detective's Notepad throughout the game to solve the case.

4. Once you think you've solved the mystery, you can make an accusation of whodunit. You can only make one in the game, so do good detective work!

What Else to Play

Check out Sleuth, another deduction game where players must figure out which one of 36 gem cards is hidden.

Did You Know?

Clue was invented in 1949 by Anthony E. Pratt in the UK and was called "Cluedo." The game has been super popular in both the US and the UK for decades, and a feature film was even made based on the game in 1985.

Played it! ☐ Rating: ☆☆☆☆☆

Date: ___/___/_____

With: _____

Notes: _____

_____

Uno

Uno is perfect for playing at parties with lots of people. Fast-paced and simple, this game is super easy to learn. Originally developed in the United States in 1971, this card game uses a specially printed deck.

How to Play

1. Players each get 7 cards while the rest of the deck is placed in a draw pile facedown. The top card is placed faceup next to it in a discard pile.

2. Players must match the card in the discard pile by either color or number. For instance, if the discard pile has a yellow 7, you have to place either a yellow card or a card with a 7 on it. (Or you can play a wild card if you have one.)

3. If you don't have a match, you have to draw a card from the draw pile. If that card can be played, then play it. Otherwise, the game moves on to the next player.

4. There are also action cards that can be played. Skip cards force the next player to lose a turn, Draw Two cards force the next player to pick up two cards, and Reverse cards reverse the direction of play.

5. As soon as players have one card left, they must yell, "Uno!" Play is over once a player gets rid of that last card. The aim of the game is to be the first player to reach 500 points, which you earn by adding up the other players' remaining cards.

What Else to Play

The games Mau Mau and Crazy Eights (page 96) are a lot like Uno and can both be played with a normal deck of cards.

Played it! ☐ Rating: ☆☆☆☆☆
Date: ___/___/_____
With: _____
Notes: _____
_____

AGE LEVEL:
8 and up

NUMBER OF PLAYERS:
2 to 10

WHAT YOU NEED:
Deck of Uno cards

WHERE TO PLAY:
Flat surface

ACTIVITY LEVEL:
Minimal

THE POINT OF THE GAME:
Get rid of all your Uno cards

GAME NO.

85

Mancala

Mancala and its many variations originated in Africa around 1,300 years ago and is still played today. The rules below are for the most popular version played in the West, Kalah.

How to Play

1. The Mancala board is made up of two rows of six holes each. Four pieces called stones are placed in each of the twelve holes. Each player has a store to the right side of the board.

2. Begin with one player picking up all the pieces in any one of the holes on his or her side. Moving counter-clockwise, the player deposits one of the stones in each hole until the stones run out. If players run across their own store, they deposit one piece in it. If they run across their opponent's store, they skip it. If the last piece they drop is in their own store, they go again.

3. Players alternate turns moving stones they pick up from holes on their side of the board. If the last stone dropped is in an empty hole on their side, they capture that piece and any pieces in the hole directly opposite. All captured pieces go into the player's store.

Tip

You don't need a Mancala board to play. Draw one on a sidewalk with chalk and collect 48 pebbles to play with. Or dig small holes in the dirt.

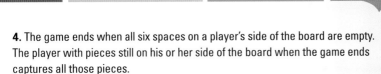

4. The game ends when all six spaces on a player's side of the board are empty. The player with pieces still on his or her side of the board when the game ends captures all those pieces.

5. Count the pieces in each store, and the player with the most pieces wins.

What Else to Play

Congkak is a Mancala game played with seven holes on each side of the board and slightly different rules. It is played in Malaysia, the Philippines, Singapore, and Thailand. Bao is a traditional Mancala board game popular in East Africa and is considered more complex than Kalah.

Played it! ☐ Rating: ☆☆☆☆☆

Date: ___ / ___ / _____

With: _____

Notes: _____

_____

Did You Know?

Mancala is actually a type of game and not a specific game. The rules here are for Kalah, the most popular version. There are more than 800 traditional Mancala games in the world.

GAME NO.

86

The Mill Game

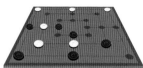

Also known as Nine Men's Morris, this is a tic-tac-toe game for people who are quickly bored by the traditional game of Tic-tac-toe.

NUMBER OF PLAYERS:
2

WHAT YOU NEED:
Mill board,
9 black pieces
and 9 white pieces

WHERE TO PLAY:
Flat surface

ACTIVITY LEVEL:
Minimal

THE POINT OF THE GAME:
Create mills to remove your opponent's pieces

How to Play

1. The game board is made up of a grid with 24 points. Each player has nine pieces, which they take turns placing on the grid, trying to get three pieces in a row either horizontally or vertically. If one player forms a mill (three in a row), that player gets to remove one of the opponent's pieces.

2. Once players place all of their pieces, they take turns moving pieces to adjacent points to create three in a row. No jumping allowed!

3. A player wins by removing enough pieces so the opposing player cannot make any mills (they have only two pieces left) or if there aren't any moves left to make. Players may not remove pieces from existing mills unless there aren't any other pieces left to take.

4. A fun variation allows a player with only three pieces left to move a piece to any vacant point during their turn.

What Else to Play

Lasker Morris is a game played on the same board but with ten pieces each. At the beginning of the game, players can choose either to place a new piece on the board or to move one of the pieces already there. This creates a more complex game.

Tip

A player can break one of their mills by moving one of the pieces and then moving it back on his or her next turn to create a new mill. You can make the move over and over again until your opponent figures out a way to stop it.

Played it! ☐ Rating: ☆☆☆☆☆
Date: ___/___/_____
With: _____
Notes: _____
_____

Pandemic

GAME NO.
87

Four deadly plagues are slowly spreading across the Earth. Can you and your friends find the cures before time runs out? Unlike most games, instead of trying to beat an opponent, you have to work together with the other players to save the day.

How to Play

The game consists of a game board of the Earth with lines connecting 48 major cities, player cards, infection cards, disease cubes, research station pieces, and player pieces. Players are given random specialties, such as the Scientist, who can cure the plagues; the Medic, who cures infections; and more. During each turn, players attempt to move to another city, remove a disease cube, build a research station, or cure one of the diseases. But watch out for the Epidemic cards, which increase the infection rate and make it that much harder to contain the plagues. If you manage to eliminate the plagues, your team wins the game. If too many cities suffer outbreaks, you lose.

What Else to Play

There are several expansions available with new cards, rule variations, and new challenges. There are also two editions of the game, the second of which introduces new characters. If that's not enough, you can also play one of the five spin-off games available.

AGE LEVEL:
8 and up

NUMBER OF PLAYERS:
2 to 4

WHAT YOU NEED:
Pandemic game

WHERE TO PLAY:
Flat Surface

ACTIVITY LEVEL:
Minimal

Played it! ☐ Rating: ☆☆☆☆☆
Date: ___/___/_____
With: _____
Notes: _____
_____

THE POINT OF THE GAME:
Cure four diseases before they cause a pandemic

GAME NO.

88

Monopoly

In Monopoly, you can be the wealthiest person on the planet! Buy, rent, and sell properties to build your empire and rule the world. While all players start out with the same amount of money, with a little strategy and a bit of luck, you can claim the monopoly of Boardwalk, Park Place, and all the rest!

How to Play

1. Set up the board and card decks, and appoint a Banker to handle the money.

2. Once the Banker distributes everyone's starting fund, each player will throw the dice and start their trip around the board.

3. As you land on properties, you can buy them if you have enough money.

4. You might also land on spaces that require you to pay rent or taxes—or even send you to jail!

5. Players make their way around the board buying and selling properties and paying rent, until players either run out of money and go bankrupt, or end up being the one with the most money at the end.

> **Tip**
> Build three houses on each property as quickly as you can. This will help you earn more money!

What Else to Play

There are tons of differently themed Monopoly games, including Disney Monopoly, Monopoly Junior, and Monopoly City.

Played it! ☐ Rating: ☆☆☆☆☆

Date: ___/___/_____

With: _____

Notes: _____

_____

Reversi

Flip that disk! It's all about strategy in this board game also known as Othello. The point is to be the player with the majority of your colored disks faceup on the board at the end of the game. Get more of your colored disks on the board by "outflanking" your opponent.

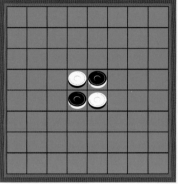

How to Play

1. Choose who will have the black disks and who will have the white. Each player gets 32 disks.
2. Play starts with two black and two white disks in the center of the board.
3. Black always goes first. On each turn, add one of your disks to the board and try to outflank your opponent. To outflank your opponent, two of your disks must surround your opponent's, boxing them in. Then you can flip the outflanked disks.
4. If you can't outflank, you forfeit your turn.
5. Play continues until neither player can move any further. Whoever is left with the most disks in their color on the board wins!

What Else to Play

Check out some other classic board games, like Backgammon (page 114) or Checkers (page 116).

Did You Know

There has been a World Othello Championship held all over the world since 1977!

Played it! ☐ Rating: ☆☆☆☆☆
Date: ___/___/_____
With: _____
Notes: _____
_____

THE POINT OF THE GAME:
Have the most disks faceup on the board

GAME NO.

90

Scattergories

In this intense, fast-thinking game, you score points for coming up with words that start with a certain letter within listed categories. But you have to think beyond the most obvious answers since you only score a point if no one else comes up with the answers you did!

How to Play

1. Each player receives a folder with an answer pad and the category lists. Each category list has 12 different categories such as U.S. Cities, Vegetables, and TV Shows.

2. One player rolls a die with the letters of the alphabet. The letter it lands on is called the key letter. At the start of the timer, each player must fill in the first column of their answer sheets. Answers must fit the category and must begin with the key letter.

3. Play ends when the timer goes off. Players then read their answers aloud and circle any answer that does not match any other player's answer. You get one point for each circled answer.

4. Play two more rounds with the same categories but with a new roll of the die. The player with the most points after all three rounds wins.

What Else to Play

Scattergories is based on the paper and pencil game Guggenheim (page 14). Also try out Facts in Five, an older game that has you draw five category cards and five letter tiles.

Tip

Score an extra point for using alliteration. For example, if you answered *The Brady Bunch* for TV shows that start with B, you'd get 2 points.

Played it! ☐ Rating: ☆☆☆☆☆

Date: ___/___/_____

With: _____

Notes: _____

_____

Game for Fame

The tagline for this hilarious party game is, "Race from rags to riches and end up in stitches!" Much like many celebrities, you won't need any special talent or skill to gain fame and fortune.

How to Play

This game is played with teams of at least two players each. The rules are quite simple, but the premise is to take on ridiculous challenges to win money and get closer to the red carpet. The teams take turns picking up Money Cards and performing the challenges on the card. For instance, one card may ask a player to imitate five accents in 60 seconds. The number of correct guesses is the number of places you move. Even though you're working in teams, it's the player with the most money at the end of the game who wins. Writing the funniest poem, singing the silliest song, and more can also earn money, which you'll need if you want to be the richest celebrity once somebody makes it to the red carpet.

What Else to Play

Like living the lifestyle of the rich and famous? Check out the game Malibu, in which you start off with $4,000,000 and pick up Fame and Fortune cards along the way. This game is silly fun for older kids, teens, and adults.

Did You Know?

This is one of the few games where you don't shuffle the cards! The cards are in numerical order and should be played in that order so that one team doesn't end up with similar types of challenges.

AGE LEVEL:
10 and up

NUMBER OF PLAYERS:
4 to 16

WHAT YOU NEED:
Game for Fame game

WHERE TO PLAY:
Anywhere

ACTIVITY LEVEL:
Minimal

THE POINT OF THE GAME:
Become the highest paid superstar

Played it! ☐ Rating: ☆☆☆☆☆

Date: ___/___/_____

With: _____

Notes: _____

_____

Scrabble

Scrabble is known as the crossword game because when you're finished, the board looks like a wild crossword puzzle. Players take turns creating interlocking words using letter tiles of different values in the hopes that at the end of the game, they will have the most points.

How to Play

1. The Scrabble game set comes with a game board, 100 letter tiles (usually wood), and four tile racks. All the letters are placed in a bag or turned facedown at the side of the board. Each player chooses seven random tiles and puts them on his or her rack so no one else can see them.

2. Combine two or more letters to form a word and place it on the board either vertically or horizontally (no diagonals allowed) with one letter on the middle star square. Add up the points on the letter tiles, announce the total to the scorekeeper, and then replace the played tiles with new tiles chosen from the bag.

3. All words are okay to use except those that are always capitalized (proper names, locales), abbreviations, prefixes and suffixes, and words requiring a hyphen or apostrophe.

4. Play continues in this manner with each player adding one or more letters to the board to form new words. During a turn, you can decide to exchange all or some of your letters for new ones. If new letters are chosen, your turn is over and you don't get to create a new word.

Tip

A general rule of thumb is to aim for one of the many premium squares on the board that give you extra points (double letter, double word, triple letter, triple word).

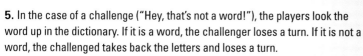

5. In the case of a challenge ("Hey, that's not a word!"), the players look the word up in the dictionary. If it is a word, the challenger loses a turn. If it is not a word, the challenged takes back the letters and loses a turn.

6. The game is over when all of the letters have been drawn and one player has used up his or her last letter—or when no more plays are possible. The player with the highest score is the winner.

What Else to Play

Bananagrams is a word game with letter tiles that come in a cloth bag in the shape of a banana. The goal is for each player to create interlocking words with the tiles. The first player to use all his or her tiles wins.

Played it! ☐ Rating: ☆☆☆☆☆

Date: ___/___/_____

With: _____

Notes: _____

_____

Did You Know?

The word "scrabble" means to scratch, claw, or grope frantically.

Settlers of Catan

Do you ever wish you could strike out on your own and build your own city? Settlers of Catan is a board game where you trade, build, and settle on the fictional island of Catan. You don't need a shovel—just a few friends and this extremely popular game that's easy to learn but takes a lot of strategic thinking to win.

How to Play

After randomly placing the large hexagonal tiles that represent natural resources on the island game board, players take turns putting up their first settlements and rolling the dice to collect, trade, and use resource cards (brick, lumber, grain, etc.). With resource cards and development cards, players build their settlements and roads.

The object is to be the first to gain 10 victory points, which you get by developing settlements (1 point each) and cities (2 points each), as well as by earning accomplishment cards, such as Longest Road and Largest Army. Watch out for the robber, though, who at the roll of a seven can come in and take what's yours.

Tip
Build your roads, cities, and settlements as quickly as possible. This makes trading easier.

What Else to Play

Once you own the base game, you can expand with Seafarers, Cities and Knights, Explorers and Pirates, or Traders and Barbarians. There are also base game expansion cards so that 5 to 6 players can play. You can also explore special stand-alone editions of the game as well as spin-offs.

Played it! ☐ Rating: ☆☆☆☆☆

Date: ___/___/_____

With: _____

Notes: _____

_____

Did You Know?

In 2015, 1,040 participants, including the game's creator, Klaus Teuber, played the largest game of Catan ever.

GAME NO.
94

Battleship

It's your fleet against the enemy's. Take turns launching attacks that get more and more accurate with each hit. Who emerges victorious depends on strategic placement of the ships and clever attacks.

How to Play
Each player receives a hinged game board with two gridded pegboards. One board is for placing your ships. The other is for plotting your attack against the enemy's ships. Each player also receives 15 miniature ships, including 1 carrier ship, 2 battleships, 3 cruisers, 4 submarines, and 5 destroyers. Once you've placed your ships on the board, alternate turns by launching attacks against your enemy's fleet. For instance, one player says, "G-3." The other player looks at the location of his or her ships and yells, "Hit!" or "Miss!" Record your hits and misses on the other pegboard. The player to sink all of the enemy's ships wins.

What Else to Play
This game is based on an old paper-and-pencil game called Sea Battle. Each player places their ships on a 10" x 10" piece of grid paper with columns numbered 1 to 10 and rows lettered A to J. Each player gets 1 carrier (5 grid boxes), 1 battleship (4 boxes), 1 cruiser (3 boxes), 2 destroyers (2 boxes each), and 2 submarines (1 box each).

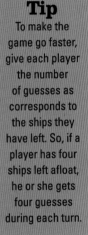

Tip
To make the game go faster, give each player the number of guesses as corresponds to the ships they have left. So, if a player has four ships left afloat, he or she gets four guesses during each turn.

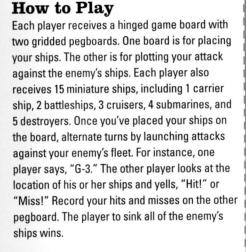

Played it! ☐ Rating: ☆☆☆☆☆
Date: ___/___/_____
With: _____
Notes: _____
_____

Mastermind

This board game relies on your deductive code-cracking skills to guess the color and position of four hidden pegs. The only hints you get are the clues your opponent gives after each turn. Are you a Mastermind?

How to Play

At the beginning of play, the Mastermind board is empty. The code maker secretly creates a pattern made from piles of six different colored pegs in a row of four holes hidden behind a screen. The code breaker then has to guess not only the colors of the pegs but also their order and position. The code breaker places a first guess in the peg holes on the board. Using smaller black and white pegs, the code maker shows the code breaker how many of the guesses are the correct color (white peg) and how many are the correct color and in the right location (black peg). With this information, the code breaker uses logic and guesswork to make a second guess. Play continues until the code is broken or the code breaker runs out of chances. Then the players switch roles and play again.

NUMBER OF PLAYERS:
2

What Else to Play

Try the paper and pencil version of Mastermind, which is called Bulls and Cows. This game uses a four-digit number code, with no repeating numbers. The code breaker has ten tries to guess the code. If a matching number is in the correct position, it's called a "bull." If the numbers match but are in an incorrect position, it's called a "cow."

WHAT YOU NEED:
Mastermind game

Did You Know?
Code makers can choose to use the same colored pegs for more than one hole.

WHERE TO PLAY:
Flat surface

Played it! ☐ Rating: ☆☆☆☆☆

Date: ___/___/_____

With: _____

Notes: _____

_____

ACTIVITY LEVEL:
Minimal

THE POINT OF THE GAME:
Guess the color and position of the hidden pegs

GAME NO.

96

Dominoes

No game closet is complete without a Dominoes set. The traditional set contains 28 tiles (called *bones*), each of which is divided in half with continuing points from 0 to 6 (called *pips*). These are the rules for the most commonly played form of Dominoes, but there are tons of different ways to play!

How to Play

1. Lay the domino tiles facedown on a table. Each player chooses 7 tiles randomly and keeps them hidden from the other players, laying them out on the long edges.

2. If playing with 2 or 3 players, the rest of the tiles are left facedown in the boneyard. If playing with 4 players, all the tiles will be in use.

3. If playing with 2 or 3 players, have one player place one tile faceup on the play area. If playing with 4 players, the player with the double-6 tile goes first by putting that tile faceup on the play area.

4. Moving counterclockwise, the next player must put down one tile with a matching end. If the first player plays a 6/6 tile, the next player must play a tile with an end that has 6 pips.

Tip

This is a game of luck and strategy. As you play, keep your attention on what tiles your opponent passes on. Use that information to your advantage when playing tiles.

5. The next player follows by placing a tile with an end that matches any open tile end. If a player cannot attach a tile, he or she must pick from the boneyard until a tile can be played. If playing with 4 players, the turn passes to the next player.

6. The round ends when a player has no more tiles. The winner is awarded points based on the number of pips on the other players' tiles. Whoever reaches 200 points first wins.

What Else to Play

Other Dominoes games to play include Bergen Dominoes, Bingo, Poker, Matadore, and more.

Played it! ☐ Rating: ☆☆☆☆☆

Date: ___/___/_____

With: _____

Notes: _____

_____

Did You Know?
Double pieces (6/6, 5/5, etc.) are placed sideways on the domino line.

GAME NO.

97

Dungeons and Dragons

In this complex and engaging game, create new identities; go on epic adventures with your friends; fight monsters, dragons, and wizards; and perhaps find a chest filled with treasure—all without leaving your dining room table.

How to Play

You can't begin a D&D adventure without a character. You build your new identity by deciding what you want to be and then rolling the dice to figure out your strengths and abilities. Meanwhile, one player is the Dungeon Master, who creates and referees the adventure and narrates the events as you experience them. You and the other adventurers then set out exploring caves, castles, and labyrinths, deciding which way to go and what to do next. Need to attack a troll that's guarding a golden sword? Roll the multi-sided die. The die along with your ability scores decide whether or not you are successful. Games can last hours, and you may reach the end with additional experience points and power. Other times, you may die. A series of games, called a "campaign," could last several sessions over the course of days or even weeks.

Tip

This game has a lot of components, but if you're just starting out, you can purchase a starter set that has everything you need to begin your first adventure. If you are looking for people to play with or to teach you to play, find out where you can buy Dungeons and Dragons materials and see if they have game nights at the store.

What Else to Play

One world not enough for you? Try these popular RPGs (role-playing games): Traveller (science fiction), GURPs (multi-genre), Savage Worlds (multi-genre), and Pathfinder (fantasy).

Played it! ☐   Rating: ☆☆☆☆☆

Date: ___/___/_____

With: _____

Notes: _____

_____

Did You Know?

Dungeons and Dragons was the first and is arguably still the best-known and best-selling role-playing game. More than 20 million people have played the game around the world and it has been featured in books, movies, and television series.

GAME NO.

98

Magic: The Gathering

AGE LEVEL:
13 and up

In Magic: The Gathering's universe, you are a powerful wizard known as a Planeswalker. You can travel the countless worlds of the Multiverse. It is your duty to battle and defeat other Planeswalkers. Are you up to the challenge?

NUMBER OF PLAYERS:
2

How to Play

Each game you play represents a battle between wizards, and like other trading card games, you first need to build your deck of cards for play. You'll need at least 60 cards for a good game. These cards are your spells and the creatures you can summon to do battle, as well as the cards needed to cast your spells. Each wizard starts off with 20 life points, and the first player to lose all their points loses. The game may seem a little unpredictable at times, since you have to play the cards you are dealt, but there's a tremendous amount of strategy and imagination needed to navigate the many rules regarding attacks.

WHAT YOU NEED:
Magic cards

WHERE TO PLAY:
Flat surface

Tip

Some stores offer free welcome decks to new players featuring two 30-card decks—all you need to start your first game!

ACTIVITY LEVEL:
Minimal

THE POINT OF THE GAME:
Defeat your opponent with your spell cards

What Else to Play

There are so many good trading card games to choose from, including Star Wars: The Card Game, Dragon Ball Z, Epic Card Game, and Legend of the Five Rings.

Played it! ☐ Rating: ☆☆☆☆☆

Date: ___/___/_____

With: _____

Notes: _____

_____

Did You Know?
There are more than 17,000 Magic: The Gathering cards you can collect to build your decks. Some Magic cards are so rare that they are worth thousands of dollars.

GAME NO.

99

Pokémon

You may know Pokémon as an anime series, a video game series, or a smartphone adventure, but it is also an incredibly popular collectible trading card game in which you create exciting Pokémon battles. When first purchasing cards, buy a themed deck. These are designed to cover the basics of the game. You can then buy booster packs to customize your playing deck. There are thousands of cards to choose from so each game is never the same.

NUMBER OF PLAYERS:
2

How to Play

Half (or more than half!) the fun of playing Pokémon is collecting the cards. These are purchased in packs. It's also fun trading cards with friends until you have the Pokémon you want and like. A full game is played with 60 cards each. Twenty of them are basic cards, which are the Pokémon you will use to do battle. Twenty are energy cards, which you use to help your Pokémon use their powers. The rest are trainer cards, which you use to do special things, such as heal Pokémon, discard opponent energy cards, retrieve cards from the discard pile, and more! You and your opponent are trainers, and once you've set up your cards, you take turns doing battle against each other. Any Pokémon that has sustained enough damage is knocked out and the opponent gets a prize card. The player who picks up all his or her prize cards first is the winner.

WHAT YOU NEED:
Pokémon game cards

WHERE TO PLAY:
Flat surface

Tip

Play a few practice rounds with an experienced player before playing a full round. The rules take some getting used to.

ACTIVITY LEVEL:
Minimal

THE POINT OF THE GAME:
Defeat your opponent's Pokémon

What Else to Play

If you like trading card games, try Yu-Gi-Oh!, Magic: The Gathering (page 136), Netrunner, World of Warcraft, and more.

Played it! ☐ Rating: ☆☆☆☆☆

Date: ___ / ___ / _____

With: _____

Notes: _____

_____

Did You Know?

Pokémon are mythical creatures of all shapes and sizes that live in the wild and are raised by their human trainers. There are more than 700 Pokémon creatures.

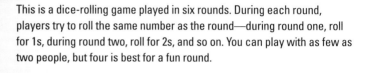

GAME NO.

100

Bunco

**AGE
LEVEL:**
6 and up

This is a dice-rolling game played in six rounds. During each round, players try to roll the same number as the round—during round one, roll for 1s, during round two, roll for 2s, and so on. You can play with as few as two people, but four is best for a fun round.

**NUMBER
OF PLAYERS:**
2 to 4

How to Play

1. Create a scorecard like the one shown.

2. During round 1, players take turns rolling the three dice at the same time for 1s. If players roll any 1s, they mark the amount on their scorecard and roll the dice again. Players keep rolling and keeping track of points until they don't roll any 1s. Then the player to the left rolls.

3. The first player to reach twenty-one 1s wins the round and records one win. The players then move to round two, where they each try to roll for 2s.

**WHAT YOU
NEED:**
Three dice for
every 4 players,
paper, pencil

4. There are some special rules. If players roll three of the same number that isn't that round's number, it's called a Binco (for example, you roll three 6s in round one). Mark a Binco in on your scorecard. If you roll three of that round's number, you get a Bunco (for example, you roll three 1s in round one). Yell "Bunco!" and you automatically win the round. The other players all mark a loss on their sheet and play moves on to the next round.

**WHERE TO
PLAY:**
Flat surface

Tip
There's really no special strategy involved. It's all the luck of the dice. That doesn't mean the game isn't fun!

**ACTIVITY
LEVEL:**
Minimal

**THE POINT
OF THE GAME:**
Win the most rounds

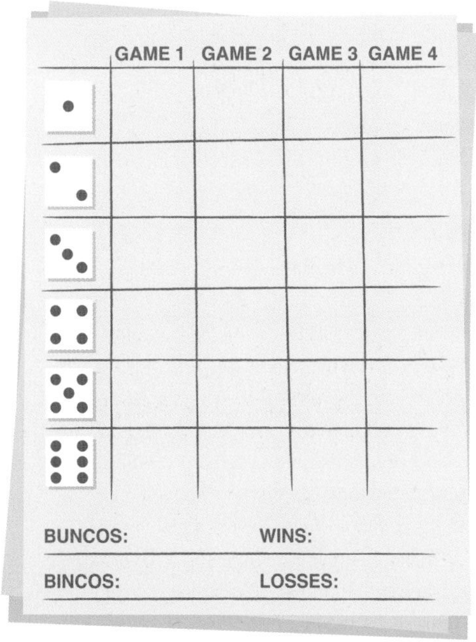

	GAME 1	GAME 2	GAME 3	GAME 4
⚀				
⚁				
⚂				
⚃				
⚄				
⚅				

BUNCOS: _____ WINS: _____

BINCOS: _____ LOSSES: _____

5. After rolling all six rounds, count up your wins and see who's the winner. If there's a tie, count your Buncos. Still tied? Count Bincos. Still tied? Have a roll-off or call it a day.

What Else to Play

Yahtzee (page 144) is a fun dice game that is mostly luck, but also has some elements of skill involved.

Played it! ☐ Rating: ☆☆☆☆☆

Date: ___ / ___ / _____

With: _____

Notes: _____

_____

Did You Know?

Giant Bunco parties with different tables of players going up against each other are a big deal, and the winners usually receive prizes.

GAME NO.
101

Yahtzee

AGE LEVEL:
6 and up

NUMBER OF PLAYERS:
2 to 10

WHAT YOU NEED:
Yahtzee game or five dice and scorecards

WHERE TO PLAY:
Flat surface

ACTIVITY LEVEL:
Minimal

THE POINT OF THE GAME:
Roll dice combinations to score the most points

This family-favorite dice-rolling game has been around for more than 60 years. It may seem like the game is all about the luck of the dice, but it actually takes brains as you strategize the best way to fill out your scorecard. And if your dice all show the same number, don't forget to yell, "Yahtzee!"

How to Play

Players take turns rolling the five dice to form the thirteen combinations that appear on the scorecard. The upper section asks for dice rolls for the numbers 1 through 6. So if you roll three sixes you place eighteen in that box. The bottom section includes poker-like combinations including four of a kind, full-house, large straight (sequence of five such as 2, 3, 4, 5, 6), and a Yahtzee (five of a kind). The game gets tricky when the dice don't cooperate and you have to make difficult decisions on how to fill in your scorecard. And if you can't roll one of the combinations, you have to put a zero in that box. The player with the highest score wins.

What Else to Play

Dice Town plays a lot like Yahtzee but has more of a poker card game feel to it.

Tip

If you have to place a zero in a category, place it in the Yahtzee box as that is the most difficult combination to get.

Did You Know?

According to Yahtzee legend, the game was invented by a Canadian couple who played it on a yacht.

Played it! ☐ Rating: ☆☆☆☆☆
Date: ___/ ___/ _____
With: _____
Notes: _____
_____